W9-CGX-764

CliffsNotes™ Using Your First PC

by Jim McCarter

IN THIS BOOK

- Connecting your PC parts
- Starting your system
- Connecting to the Internet
- Keeping your system in tip-top shape
- Reinforce what you learn with CliffsNotes Review
- Find more computing information in CliffsNotes Resource Center and online at www.cliffsnotes.com

IDG Books Worldwide, Inc.
An International Data Group Company

Foster City, CA • Chicago, IL • Indianapolis, IN • New York, NY

IDG BOOKS WORLDWIDE

About the Author

Jim McCarter has trained computer users and designed computer systems for over ten years.

Publisher's Acknowledgments

Editorial

Senior Project Editor: Pat O'Brien

Acquisitions Editor: Steve Hayes

Copy Editor: Ted Cains

Technical Editor: Phil Robertson, Bob Correll

Production

Proofreader: Chris Collins

Indexer: Johnna VanHoose

IDG Books Indianapolis Production Department

Table of Contents

INTRODUCTION

Congratulations! Owning your first PC is an exciting milestone. Whether you want to use your PC for work, for school, or for fun, it's a powerful tool.

Your new PC may be fresh from the manufacturer or passed to you from another happy user who wanted more performance. Either way, CliffsNotes *Using Your First PC* guides you through the essentials of getting started with your new system.

Why Do You Need This Book?

Can you answer yes to any of these questions?

- Do you need to learn about your PC fast?

- Don't have time to read 500 pages about your new computer?

- Want to access the Internet in record time?

- Want to keep your system running smoothly?

If so, then CliffsNotes *Using Your First PC* is for you!

How to Use This Book

CliffsNotes *Using Your First PC* is a fast, cover-to-cover introduction to the world of PC ownership. I've organized the chapters in a logical progression intended to get you up, running, and doing real things with your computer in very short order.

If your system is already connected, you won't need to follow the connection instructions at the beginning of the book. To find out whether a chapter is useful today, read its introduction. The introductions are brief and tell you whether the chapter is of particular interest to you.

As you proceed through the book, the following icons identify paragraphs of particular interest:

Think of these paragraphs as the essential truths you must remember.

Be wary! You can create big problems if you ignore this advice.

Impress your friends and confound your enemies with these gems.

Don't Miss Our Web Site

Keep up with the changing world of computing by visiting the CliffsNotes Web site at www.cliffsnotes.com. Here's what you find there:

- Interactive tools that are fun and informative
- Links to interesting Web sites
- Additional resources to help you continue your learning

At the CliffsNotes Web site, you can even register for a new feature called *CliffsNotes Daily*, which offers you newsletters on a variety of topics, delivered right to your e-mail inbox each business day.

If you haven't yet discovered the Internet and are wondering how to get online, pick up *Getting On the Internet*, new from CliffsNotes. You learn just what you need to make your online connection quickly and easily. See you at www.cliffsnotes.com!

CHAPTER 1

TAKING INVENTORY

IN THIS CHAPTER

- System unit — the box that holds the "guts" of the PC

- Monitor — looks like a small TV set

- Keyboard and mouse — these guys let you tell the PC what to do

- Printers — lets you put the information down on paper

Now that you've finally acquired your first PC, the two of you should become acquainted. This chapter introduces you to the basic components that all PCs share, as well as some of the more common add-on peripherals. (Chapter 3 explains how to connect the pieces.)

Almost all PCs have these basic components:

- System unit (box full of electronics)

The system unit holds the Windows *operating system* (software that tells the hardware what to do). The operating system is essential. If you've already seen someone else use your computer, the operating system is installed. If you haven't seen anyone use your computer, ask whether Windows is installed.

If you're new to computing, I don't recommend trying to install the Windows operating system yourself. When you buy a new PC, insist on having Windows installed at the store before you take it home. If your PC is a gift or a hand-me-down, politely ask your benefactor to install it or recommend someone else to do so.

Operating systems, like most software, are generally licensed for use on one computer at a time. This means that if you don't have an operating system for your PC, you can't legally make a copy of your friend's operating system and install it on your computer.

■ Monitor (like a TV set)

■ Keyboard (like the keys of a typewriter)

■ Mouse (or other pointing device)

After reading this chapter, you should be able to readily identify these computer components. You'll also be able to determine whether you have all the necessary PC components to start using the computer.

System Unit

The *system unit* contains the guts of your computer system. Just about everything in the system unit is important for the operation of your computer, but most pieces you never see or touch. This section covers those components that you will interact with. Here they are:

■ **Hard disk:** This device stores all your programs and data. Information that you store on a disk drive is not lost when you turn off the computer. Most hard disk drives are measured in gigabytes and megabytes. A gigabyte (GB) is equal to 1024 megabytes (MB). Some PCs have 18GB hard disks. The bigger your hard disk drive, the more software programs and information you can store on your computer.

Usually, a light flashes on the front of your system unit or you may hear a little noise when your computer is accessing the hard disk.

■ **Floppy disk drive:** You can use the floppy disk, like the hard disk, to store programs and data. Floppy disks are much slower and have a far smaller capacity than a hard disk.

The floppy's main advantage is that it lets you easily copy information from one computer to another. You can also use this disk to make a spare copy of your computer work, in case you damage your computer or accidentally delete your work.

■ **CD-ROM (Compact Disc-Read Only Memory) drive:** This type of drive uses CDs (which look just like music CDs) to hold programs and data.

Most new software programs come on CD-ROM. If you want to add a computer program at home, you probably need a CD-ROM drive. Even if you don't plan to add programs, you may need a CD-ROM drive to install software for such devices as printers.

Unless you have a special CD drive (and special CDs), you can't record on a CD. You can only play it.

■ **Video card:** The video card is a set of electronics that is responsible for displaying text and images on the monitor. Without a video card, you can't plug in a monitor.

■ **Sound card:** This set of electronics allows your computer to play sounds and music.

The sound card starts with digital information, which you can't hear, and changes it to the same kind of signal that speakers use. When you connect a speaker to the sound card, you hear the computer.

You probably need *amplified* speakers to hear your computer. Basic amplified speakers are inexpensive, if you don't already have them.

Usually, a PC has a simple sound card. It won't sound as good as a home stereo system, even with expensive speakers. If you want to rattle the windows when you play computer games, you can spend hundreds of dollars on your computer sound card, amplifier, and speakers — just like a stereo system.

■ **Modem:** This allows your computer to communicate with other computers via the telephone line.

The modem is the most common method of connecting to the Internet.

System units come in a variety of shapes, sizes, and even colors.

■ The most common system unit is the *desktop,* which usually sits on the desk (hence the name) next to or under the monitor. Figure 1-1 shows a desktop system.

Figure 1-1:   Common PC components.

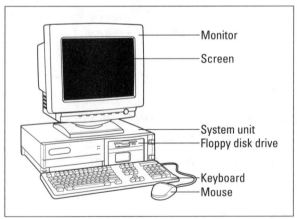

■ Many new computers come in a *tower* configuration. Tower computers help alleviate some of the clutter on your desk and usually sit on the floor.

No matter which type of system unit you have — desktop or tower — they all function essentially the same.

Remember

If you have a portable computer, you can forget about the desktop versus tower business. Portable computers — or *laptops* — have the system unit, monitor, and keyboard all in one unit. Most new portable computers are called *notebooks* because, when closed, they're about the size of a notebook, albeit a thick notebook. Some new portables, known as *ultra-portables,* weigh less than three pounds and fit easily into a briefcase. Portable computers can have the same components as their larger desktop and tower brethren. The difference is mainly in the size of the components. In order to be portable, the components in the portable computer must be smaller and lighter.

On the front of most PCs, you find the following:

- **Power switch:** Turns the PC on or off. (This switch may be on the side or back).

- **Reset button:** Restarts the PC without turning it off and back on.

- **Floppy disk drive:** Receives floppy disks to copy files.

- **CD-ROM drive:** Receives CDs to play music, play games, or install software.

- **Status lights:** Indicates the status of various aspects of the system unit, such as power on or off, hard drive activity, floppy drive activity, and CD-ROM drive activity.

- **Sleep button:** Puts PC in standby mode or wakes PC from standby mode.

Monitor

The *monitor* is the part of your PC that looks like a TV set. There are two basic types of monitors available today:

- Cathode-ray tube (like most TV sets).

    Most desktop and tower computers use a CRT monitor.

- Flat panel LCD (like a picture frame).

    Most portable computers use an LCD screen.

Monitor screens are measured in *size* and *resolution.*

- Size is the width of the screen measured diagonally from corner to corner. For example, a screen 12 inches wide and 9 inches high measures 15 inches diagonally from corner to corner.

    Screen size determines how *big* the picture can be.

- Resolution is the number of horizontal rows and vertical columns of *pixels* the monitor is capable of displaying.

    A pixel, or picture element, is a small dot on the screen that can be turned on or off, or set to display a particular color. All monitors are capable of displaying at least 640 x 480 pixels. Some are capable of up to 1600 x 1200 resolution.

    Screen resolution determines how *detailed* the picture can be.

The monitor, regardless of the type, plugs into a video adapter in the system unit. The video adapter may be part of the system board, or it may be a separate *expansion card* that plugs into the system board. You probably never need to know whether your video adapter is built-in.

Most monitors have brightness and contrast controls, usually located on the front. Many monitors also have controls for horizontal and vertical size and position, so you can put the picture exactly in the center of the screen.

CRT monitors

CRT stands for Cathode Ray Tube and is the same technology used in television sets. The larger the monitor, the larger your picture looks, just like a TV set.

Lots of people find 17-inch monitors are a good compromise for space, screen size, and price. If you already have a 14-inch or 15-inch monitor, you probably don't need to run out and buy a bigger one.

LCD monitors

LCD stands for Liquid Crystal Display. Until recently, LCD monitors were found almost exclusively in portable computers. LCD monitors provide a crisp, flicker-free image that puts less strain on your eyes. Aside from the ergonomic benefits, LCD monitors weigh much less, take up less desktop real estate, and consume less electricity than their CRT cousins.

A big LCD monitor for a desktop or tower computer is a pretty expensive item. If you're worried about the space a CRT monitor takes on your desk, you'll probably find a bigger desk is cheaper than a big LCD monitor.

Keyboard

The *keyboard* is the computer's primary input device for typing letters and numbers.

You don't need to know about the keyboard right away. You can skip this section for now and come back later.

If you have ever used a typewriter, most of the keys on the keyboard are probably familiar to you. The keys can be divided into five categories.

Alphanumeric keys

The alphanumeric keys consist of the standard letter keys (A – Z), and the number keys located in a row above the letters.

The alphanumeric keys also include punctuation, such as periods and commas.

Function keys

The function keys, labeled F1 through F12, are usually located in a row along the top of the keyboard. (Older keyboards may have the function keys located in two vertical columns along the left side of the keyboard. These older keyboards usually have only ten function keys.)

The purpose of the functions keys depends on what you are doing with your computer. For example, pressing the F1 key makes the Help system appear on the screen in most Microsoft programs.

Cursor movement keys

These keys consist of four *arrow* keys and the Home, End, Page Up, and Page Down keys. The exact function of these keys varies depending on the application that you are currently using. Generally, pressing an arrow key causes the *cursor* (the blinking line where your typing appears) to move in the direction of the arrow. Pressing the Page Up key causes the screen to scroll up one screen; Page Down causes the screen to scroll down one screen. Pressing Home or End causes the cursor to move to the beginning or end of a line, respectively.

Numeric keypad

The numeric keypad mimics a standard 10-key calculator. It consists of

■ Numbers 0 through 9

■ The decimal point

■ The Enter key

■ Basic math functions ('-', '+', '/', and '*')

■ The Num Lock key

The Num Lock key functions like a toggle switch. Press the key once to turn the Num Lock feature on, press it a second time to turn the feature off. On most keyboards, an indicator lights up to let you know that the Num Lock feature is turned on. When the Num Lock feature is turned on, the keys function like those on a 10-key calculator.

Usually, the keys on the numeric keypad are overlaid with the names of the cursor movement keys. When the Num Lock feature is turned off, the number keys become cursor movement keys.

Most portable computers don't have a separate numeric keypad. Usually, some of the letters on the keyboard serve as the numeric keypad. The Num Lock key changes this section of the keyboard from letters to numbers.

Miscellaneous keys

As you have probably surmised, these are the keys that do not fall into any of the other four categories:

- Esc

  Located in the top-left corner of the keyboard, the Esc (Escape) key usually cancels the current operation.

- Print Screen

  On Windows PCs, pressing this key causes the picture on the screen to be copied to the Windows *clipboard* (a special part of the computer's memory). Pictures and words in the clipboard can be added into documents when your PC is running.

- Scroll Lock

  Most of the time, this key serves no purpose. In some programs, such as Microsoft Excel, pressing Scroll Lock turns the arrow keys into scroll keys. Instead of moving the cursor from cell to cell, the arrow keys scroll the entire worksheet.

  Scroll Lock is a toggle key. Press it once to turn it on, press it again to turn it off. On some keyboards, a light comes on to indicate that the feature is turned on.

- Pause/Break

  This key is a holdover from DOS and isn't much use in Windows.

- Tab

  When you type on your PC, the tab key moves the cursor a preset distance to the right, like the tab key on a typewriter.

- Shift

  The Shift key allows you to type capital letters. Hold the Shift key down while typing the desired letter. The Shift key also lets you access the symbols indicated above the numbers on the number keys. Most keyboards have two Shift keys.

- Caps Lock

  This key functions like the Shift Lock key on a type-writer, with the exception that it doesn't affect the number keys. With the Caps Lock feature turned on, you can type capital letters without holding down the Shift key. (With Caps Lock on, holding down the Shift key makes letters lower case.)

  Remember

  This is a toggle key. Press it once to turn it on, press it again to turn it off. On some keyboards, a light comes on to indicate that Caps Lock is turned on.

- Ctrl

  By itself, the Ctrl (Control) key doesn't do anything. Used in conjunction with other keys, the Ctrl key *modifies* the function of the other key. For example, pressing Ctrl and the letter C while you're typing copies selected words to the Windows clipboard. (Most keyboards have two Ctrl keys. Both keys do the same thing.)

- Alt

  By itself, the Alt (Alternate) key doesn't do anything. Like the Ctrl key, you hold down the Alt key to modify the function of another key.

- Insert

  Toggles between Insert and Typeover mode.

- Delete

  Erases the selected text.

- Windows

  This is the key with the Windows 95/98 logo. Pressing this key causes the Start menu to appear. This is the same as clicking the Start button on the Windows taskbar. This key does not appear on all keyboards.

- Menu

  This is the key with the picture of a menu and the arrow pointer. Pressing this key causes the context menu to appear. This is the same as clicking the right mouse button.

Mouse

The *mouse* is a small device with two or three buttons on top and a small ball embedded in its underbelly. A typical mouse, as shown in Figure 1-2, is usually attached to the back of the computer via a cable. If your mouse doesn't have a cable, it probably communicates with the system unit via infrared — just like your television remote. Sliding the mouse on a flat surface causes the ball to roll; when the mouse ball rolls, the computer moves the mouse pointer on the screen. Some new mice use optical tracking for more precise control of the mouse pointer. These mice require — and usually come with — a special mouse pad. The mouse pointer is a small white arrow that appears on the screen.

Figure 1-2: A typical two-button mouse. This mouse also has a *wheel* between the buttons; you don't need the wheel for most PC tasks.

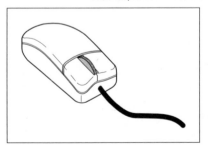

A three-button mouse is for people who like to customize how their PCs work. If you have a three-button mouse, you can ignore the center mouse button unless someone has customized your PC to use the center button.

Trackball

Some systems have a trackball in place of a mouse. The *trackball* is sort of an inverted mouse. Instead of a ball in its underside, it has a ball on top. You roll the ball with your fingers or palm instead of sliding the mouse around the desktop. Otherwise, it functions just like a mouse. Trackballs are useful where desk space is very limited. Many older portable computers have trackballs.

Touchpad

Many newer portable computers have a touchpad in place of a mouse. The *touchpad* consists of a square of pressure sensitive material and two buttons. The square represents the screen. You move the mouse cursor by sliding your finger on the touchpad. The buttons function just like those found on a mouse. Touchpads, while not common, are available for the desktop computer.

Printer

The *printer* is that thing that lets you put words and pictures from your computer on paper. Printers come in three basic varieties — almost always beige.

Inkjet printer

The type of printer that you are most likely to have is an *inkjet printer.* This type of printer creates the image on the page by spraying ink onto the paper. Inkjet printers are quiet and pretty fast. Inkjets can produce letter quality text and high-resolution graphics.

Most new inkjet printers can print in full color. Check whether yours can.

Laser printer

Laser printers are generally faster than inkjet printers. They print an entire page at a time, whereas inkjet printers print a line at a time.

Not long ago, laser printers were found almost exclusively in large office environments due to their high cost. Today, laser printers are available for under $300.

Warning

Most laser printers print only one color — black. Full-color laser printers are available, but they are significantly more expensive than color inkjet printers.

Dot-matrix printer

Dot-matrix printers aren't very common anymore, but you may just have one. Dot-matrix printers print by striking a ribbon placed between the print element and the paper. Dot-matrix printers are slow and noisy.

Tip

The most common use for this type of printer is for multi-part (carbon) forms, because dot-matrix printers strike the paper. Laser and inkjet printers don't strike the paper, so they can't use carbon-copy forms. You can print extra copies with a laser or inkjet printer.

CHAPTER 2

TAKING INVENTORY OF THE EXTRAS

IN THIS CHAPTER

- Modem — connect to the Internet
- Joystick — turn your PC into a video arcade
- CD/CD-R/CD-RW/DVD drives — store programs, music, even movies
- Removable media storage — take your data with you
- Tape backup unit — safeguard your data
- Uninterruptible power supply — provide "clean" power to your computer
- Sound card and speakers — play sounds and music
- Scanner — capture documents and photos on your PC
- Digital camera — take photographs without film

This chapter introduces you to the most popular peripheral components found on today's PCs. Don't be alarmed if your computer doesn't have all these components. You may not want or need them. And you can always add them if you wish.

After reading this chapter, you should be able to identify the most popular peripherals. Even if your computer doesn't have these devices, you can gain a basic understanding of their functions.

Modems

Modems are devices that let computers communicate with one another using telephone lines. Modems are *internal* (inside the system unit) or *external* (in a separate box that connects to the system unit).

You know that you have an internal modem if you see *phone jacks* on the back of your system unit. External modems connect to the back of the system unit via a serial cable to the serial port. Internal and external modems function identically — the only real difference is that one is installed inside the system unit and draws its power from the computer; the other connects to the back of the system unit and must plug into a power source.

You most commonly use a modem to connect your computer to the Internet via an *Internet service provider* (ISP). When your PC is connected and running, refer to Chapter 5 for more information about accessing the Internet.

Joysticks

A *joystick* is an input device used to control the computer in place of the mouse. It looks like a control stick for an airplane.

You most often use joysticks with fast-action computer games. Most games allow you to use the mouse, but you may find that you have better control and can enjoy the game more if you use a joystick.

CD-ROM Drives

A *CD-ROM* (Compact Disc — Read Only Memory) disc can hold about 650MB of data. Currently, four types of CD-ROM drives are available.

■ Standard CD-ROM drives can read prerecorded CDs. Most new software programs come on CD. These drives can also play music CDs, provided you have a sound card and speakers.

■ *DVD* drives enable you to read from the new DVD — digital versatile disc — media. DVD discs can hold about eight times the amount of data that a standard CD-ROM disc holds. The most popular use for DVDs is to play movies. DVD drives can also read standard CD-ROM discs.

■ *CD-R* drives enable you to record — hence the *R* — once to CD-R disc. You can record either computer files or music to the CD-R disc. If you make a mistake while recording or want to change the information on the disc, you must record to a new disk. CD-R drives can read standard CD-ROM discs.

■ *CD-RW* drives enable you to record multiple times to a CD-RW disc — the *RW* stands for rewritable. You can record on a CD-RW up to 1,000 times. CD-RW drives can read standard CD-ROM and CD-R discs.

Most recordable CD drives require you to use special software; putting a file on a recordable CD isn't as easy as putting a file on a floppy disk. If you're interested in using recordable CDs, wait until you're confident that you can perform basic PC tasks.

Removable Media Storage Devices

Removable media storage devices come in various shapes and sizes, but they all have some things in common.

■ They hold 100MB or more per disk.

■ They are slower than hard disks.

■ You can remove the disk for storage or to transfer to another computer.

Removable media drives, like modems, can be in the system unit or in a separate box connected by a cable.

External removable media drives can connect to the parallel port, a USB port, or to a SCSI card installed in the system unit. If you buy an external removable drive, be sure your PC has the appropriate connection.

Some external removable media drives can connect between your PC and other external devices, such as printers. Chapter 3 covers this connection

Tape Backup Units

You use *tape backup units* to make a copy of the contents of your computer's hard drive. From the tapes, you can restore files that you accidentally delete from the hard drive or that are damaged or lost due to a hard drive crash.

Tape backup drives may come installed in the system unit or may be external.

Tape backup units mostly are for organizations that automatically back up many gigabytes of data. For personal use, a removable disk drive is an adequate tool.

Surge Protector

A *surge protector* keeps very large electrical fluctuations, such as lightning strikes, from damaging your computer. You plug your PC's power cords into the surge protector, then plug the surge protector into the wall socket.

Modems are subject to damage over phone lines, too. Look for a surge protector that has jacks for your phone line.

Uninterruptible Power Supply

An *uninterruptible power supply* (UPS) is essentially a battery that delivers constant power to the computer if the building electricity varies. A UPS can also store enough power to enable you to shut down the computer properly if the electricity shuts off.

Some UPS devices come with a cable and special software that enables a computer to shut down automatically without crashing in the event of a power failure. This feature is valuable for businesses if a computer is expected to run nights and weekend without anyone to take care of it.

Sound Card and Speakers

In order to play music and sounds on your computer, you need a *sound card* and *speakers*. You install the sound card in the system unit. The speakers plug into the sound card at the back of the computer. Speakers are usually external, but you may attach them to the monitor.

If your system has a CD-ROM drive but no sound card, you may still be able to play music CDs on your computer. Check the front of the CD-ROM drive (or the back if you have an external CD-ROM drive) for a socket labeled Speakers, Audio Out, or Line Out. Plug your speakers into the port, place a music CD into the drive, and enjoy the music.

Scanners

Scanners capture printed documents or pictures and save them on your computer. After you capture your documents or pictures, you can

- Change them
- Print them
- Add them to your documents
- Post them on your Web site
- E-mail them to family and friends.

Two types of scanners are available.

- *Flatbed scanners* look like small copy machines. You place your document face down on the glass, close the cover, and tell the scanner software to copy the document to your computer.

Flatbed scanners are the best choice for copying large pictures.

- *Hand-held scanners* work by moving them over the page of your document.

Hand-held scanners are tough to use when you're trying to copy pictures wider than the scanner. To piece the result together, you have to stitch strips together electronically with your computer.

Digital Cameras

Digital cameras enable you to take photographs without using film. The camera stores the pictures on a small memory card. The number of pictures that you can take at one time depends on the picture quality and the size of the memory card. After you transfer the pictures to your computer, you can edit them, print them, post them to a Web site, or send them via e-mail.

The most common method of transferring the pictures to the computers is via a special cable that connects the camera to the serial port. Some digital cameras store pictures on a floppy disk, enabling you to transfer the pictures to the computer by simply placing the floppy disk in your floppy disk drive and using standard file management techniques.

CHAPTER 3

GETTING EVERYTHING CONNECTED

IN THIS CHAPTER

- Connecting the monitor
- Connecting the keyboard and mouse
- Connecting the printer
- Plugging in the power cords

This chapter shows you how to connect all the parts so that you can begin using your computer. Keep in mind that your computer may not have all the components mentioned in this chapter.

If you read Chapters 1 and 2, you should be familiar with the various components that make up your computer. If you don't think you can identify your PC's components, please go back to Chapters 1 and 2.

All the components listed in this chapter plug into the back of most PCs. Here's what you may find on the back of your PC's system unit:

- **Video port** to connect monitor
- **Keyboard port**
- **Mouse port** for mouse, trackball, or other pointing device
- **Serial port(s)** to connect typical external modems
- **Parallel port** for printers and other parallel port devices

- **USB port** for any device with a USB connection

- **AC power**

- **Phone jack** for internal modem

- **Sound card** to connect speakers

- **Game port** to connect joystick, steering wheel, or other game controller

Before connecting any components to the system unit, make sure that you unplug the system unit. Older systems in particular are vulnerable to damage caused by plugging in components while the system is turned on.

Connecting the Monitor

Before you connect the monitor to the system unit, take a minute to find a comfortable spot for it on your desk.

- Place the monitor where you want it before connecting it to your system. This way, you won't accidentally damage the cables or connectors by moving the monitor after it's connected.

- To avoid neck strain, you probably need to *raise* the monitor from the desktop.

Try a phone book (if you live in Manhattan, New York City) or five (if you live in Manhattan, Kansas) to raise your monitor.

The monitor comes with two cables.

- The female end of the *power cable* plugs into the back of the monitor; the male end plugs into the power outlet.

If you have a surge protector, plug your monitor's power cable into the surge protector, not a wall socket.

Make sure that you plug the power cable into a three-prong, *grounded* outlet.

■ The *signal cable* probably is permanently attached to the monitor. The other end of the signal cable plugs into the video port on the back of the system unit. The video port is a 15-pin, D-shaped female connector that is usually marked by a monitor icon. Look for a connector with three rows of five holes.

Connecting the Keyboard

The keyboard plugs into the keyboard port on the back of the system unit. Look for a keyboard icon next to a small, round connector.

Be careful not to plug the keyboard into the mouse port — the keyboard and mouse ports usually are both the same size.

Connecting the Mouse

Your mouse connection may be one of several types.

■ If your mouse has a small, round connector like the one on your keyboard, you need to plug it into the *mouse port* on the back of the system unit. Look for a mouse icon next to a small, round connector.

Be careful not to plug the mouse into the keyboard port — the mouse and keyboard ports probably are both the same size.

■ If your mouse has a D-shaped female connector with nine holes in it, you have a *serial port* mouse. Plug it into the serial port on the back of the system unit. The serial port on the system unit is a 9-pin, D-shaped male connector.

■ If you have a new *USB* mouse, plug its cable into the small, rectangular connector on the back of the system unit.

Other pointing devices, such as trackballs and touchpads, usually have one of the three types of connectors mentioned above: mouse port, serial port, or USB.

Connecting Speakers

Speaker systems usually have a Y-shaped cable with two plugs on one end — for the left and right speakers — and a single plug on the other end. The single plug connects to a port on the sound card on the back of the system unit. This port usually is labeled "Speaker" or "Line Out."

Your speakers probably have a *power* connection. Usually, a *power supply* for the speakers plugs directly into a wall socket. A cord from the power supply connects to one of your speakers. This speaker usually has the amplifier for both speakers, plus volume controls and other switches.

Connecting a Modem

Modems may be internal or external. You know that you have an internal modem if you see two phone jacks on the back of your system unit.

External modems connect to the back of the system unit via a serial cable to the serial port. The serial cable has two 9-pin, D-shaped connectors — one female and one male. The male end of the cable connects to the modem; the female end connects to the serial port on the back of the system unit. External modems also have a power supply that needs to be plugged into a wall power outlet.

Whether you have an internal or external modem, the modem has two phone jacks. Using a standard telephone cable, plug one end into the wall jack and the other end into the phone jack on the modem labeled "Line" or "Telco."

If you want to use a phone at your desk when you aren't using the modem, plug the telephone cable from the phone into the jack labeled "Phone" on the back of the modem.

Connecting a Printer

No matter what type of printer you have — inkjet, laser, or dot matrix — you probably connect it to the PC with a *parallel* printer cable.

■ One end of the parallel cable has a 25-pin, D-shaped male connector that plugs into the matching female printer port on the back of the system unit.

■ The other end of the printer cable is a D-shaped male Centronics connector, which looks like a bar with blue or gold teeth. This end plugs into the back of the printer.

■ Most printers have retainer clips that help hold the parallel printer cable neatly in place.

USB printers are different animals when it comes to connecting them to your PC. USB printers connect to the system unit with a USB cable.

■ One end of the USB cable has a square connector.

Plug the square connector into the USB connector on the back of the printer.

■ The other end of the USB cable has a rectangular connector.

Plug the rectangular end into the USB connector on the back of the system unit.

Some printers use a standard three-prong power cable. Others use a power supply similar to that used with external modems. Either way, one end plugs into a wall socket. The other end plugs into the printer (if it isn't permanently connected to the printer).

You may need to install *software* on your PC for your printer. Usually, you receive a floppy disk or CD-ROM with your printer. Connect your printer now, then install the software for the printer after your PC is up and running. Chapter 9 covers the details of installing printer software.

Connecting a Joystick

A joystick is an input device used to control the computer in place of a mouse. Joysticks are most often used with fast action computer games.

Plug the joystick cable into the *game port* on the back of the system unit. The game port is a 15-pin, D-shaped female connector with one row of eight holes and one row of seven holes.

Connecting a Removable Media Storage Device

Removable media storage devices, such as Iomega Zip drives, usually connect to the *parallel port* on the back of the computer.

External removable media storage devices usually have *two* 25-pin, D-shaped connectors — one male and one female. Here's how to attach a storage device to your system unit:

1. Connect the female end of the parallel port cable to the male connector on the storage device.

2. Connect the male end of the parallel port cable to the parallel port on the system unit. Your storage device is now connected to the system unit.

3. Connect the power cable to the storage device and a power outlet. Most drives have a power cable with a small, round connector that plugs into the back of the storage device. The other end has a standard two-prong plug that plugs into a wall socket.

Don't be surprised if your removable media drive doesn't have a power switch. Many don't.

Some removable media storage devices use USB connectors instead of parallel port cables. Just connect the square end of the USB cable to the USB port on the device and the rectangular end to the USB port on the back of the system unit.

Most removable media storage devices enable you to *daisy-chain* a printer and your device so that you can use both the device and the printer at the same time. That's why the devices come with two D-shaped connectors. Daisy-chaining simply means connecting several devices to each other in a row; for example, you can connect a printer to a Zip drive, and then connect the Zip drive to the system unit. Although you have a Zip drive between your system unit and printer, you still have no problem printing.

To daisy-chain a printer, follow the preceding numbered steps to connect the device to your system unit, then plug the 25-pin, D-shaped male end of the parallel printer cable to the female connector of the external storage device.

Connecting a Tape Backup Unit

Tape backup units typically use either a parallel port connection or a USB connection. Refer to the preceding section for how to connect a tape backup unit to your PC.

Connecting a Universal Power Supply (UPS) or Surge Protector

Connecting a UPS usually is pretty simple. Basically, it's like using a big extension cord.

1. Plug the power cable from the UPS or surge protector into a wall socket.

2. Plug the power cables from your computer and monitor into the power outlets on the UPS or surge protector.

3. If your UPS or surge protector has phone-line protection, follow its instructions to connect your modem line.

A UPS won't let you keep working indefinitely if your power is out. If the house lights don't come back on, shut down your computer until they do.

CHAPTER 4

GETTING TO KNOW MICROSOFT WINDOWS

IN THIS CHAPTER

- Starting Windows
- Launching programs from the Start menu
- Getting help from Windows
- Shutting down Windows

A computer would be an overpriced paperweight if not for the operating system. A computer without an operating system is like a car without gasoline — sure, it looks good sitting in your driveway, but you don't get much use from it.

This chapter provides a brief introduction to Windows 95 and its recent upgrade Windows 98. Both operating systems provide essentially the same functionality. Windows 98, however, offers some enhanced features that are beyond the scope of this book. Therefore, in giving you the basics, I refer to Windows 95 and Windows 98 as simply Windows.

Starting Windows

Windows is known as a GUI (which stands for graphical user interface and is pronounced "gooey") operating system. All that means is that instead of having to type arcane commands to tell the computer what to do, you point at pictures — called *icons* — and click with a pointing device — usually a mouse. Windows works as the liaison between you and your computer's hardware. You tell Windows what you want the computer to do — such as launching a program — and Windows tells the hardware what to do.

To start Windows, all you have to do is turn on the computer. Make sure you turn on the monitor and any external peripherals before you turn on the computer. After a few moments of whirring and clicking, Windows leaps to the screen and you see the Windows desktop, as shown in Figure 4-1.

Figure 4-1: The Windows desktop on your screen.

If the Welcome to Windows dialog box appears when you start Windows, type your user name and password in the boxes and click OK. If you don't know your user name and password, just press the Esc key. Windows continues to load and you soon see the Windows desktop.

Manipulating Windows

One of the great strengths of Windows is its ability to run more than one program at a time. Each program runs in its own window. You can move individual windows around on the screen. You can also resize a window to take up the entire screen, or any portion thereof.

Although you can have many windows open on the screen at one time, only one of them can be active at a time. The active window usually has a dark blue title bar — the bar at the top of the window that lists the program name. I say "usually" because you can change the colors that Windows uses to suit your preference. To make a window active, simply click anywhere inside the window with the left mouse button. If the window is partially hidden by other windows, it jumps to the top of the stack

You can resize a window in any of several ways. To enlarge the window so that it takes up the entire screen, click the Maximize button — the button that looks like a box — located in the upper-right corner of the window. The window expands to take up the entire screen, covering up the Windows desktop.

To restore a window to its previous size, click the Restore button — the button that looks like two boxes — located in the upper-right corner of the window. The window shrinks back to its previous size.

In addition to clicking the Maximize and Restore buttons, you can resize a window by dragging any of its borders inward to shrink the window or outward to enlarge the window. Keep in mind that this procedure only works with windows that you haven't maximized. Point the mouse pointer at a border of the window until the pointer turns into a double arrow. Click and hold down the left mouse button and drag the border in or out to shrink or enlarge the window. To adjust the width of the window, drag the left or right border. To adjust the height of the window, drag the top or bottom border. Drag a corner border to adjust both the width and height simultaneously.

If you resize a window such that the monitor can't display all its contents, scroll bars appear to the right and/or bottom of the window. To display the portion of the document not currently visible in the window, click the arrows in the scroll bar. Clicking the arrow at the bottom of the scroll bar moves the text up so that you can see what lies below the current screen. Clicking the up arrow at the top of the scroll bar moves the text down so that you can see what is above the current screen.

If the window is too narrow to display its contents, you can use the scroll bar located at the bottom of the window to scroll left and right. Figure 4-2 identifies a plethora of on-screen controls.

To move a window, simply drag it by its title bar.

To close a window, click the *X* in the upper-right corner of the window. When you close a window, you lose any information in the window that you haven't saved to disk. Most programs give you an option to save your work before the document closes; your best bet is to always click Yes.

If you want to get a window out of the way without closing it, you can minimize it to a button on the Windows taskbar. Click the button with the dash in the upper-right corner of the window. The window disappears from the screen. To resurrect the window, just click on its button in the taskbar. For more on the taskbar, see "Tackling the Taskbar" later in this chapter.

Figure 4-2: Windows on-screen controls.

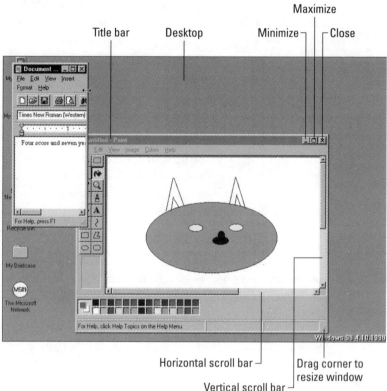

Title bar · Desktop · Maximize · Minimize · Close

Horizontal scroll bar · Drag corner to resize window

Vertical scroll bar

Starting Programs from the Start Menu

Starting programs in Windows couldn't be easier. Just click the Start button — located in the lower-left corner of the screen — to make the Start menu pop onto the screen. Point at Programs to see its submenu; if you see the program that you want to run, just place your cursor over the name of the folder, which causes yet another submenu to appear, and then click the name of the program. Figure 4-3 shows this progression of menus.

Figure 4-3: The Start menu.

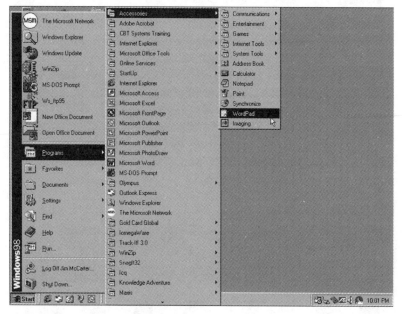

Tackling the Taskbar

The Windows taskbar, located at the bottom of the screen, helps you keep track of all your open windows. In addition to the Start button, the taskbar contains a button for each currently opened program and document on your computer.

To quickly switch from one window to another, click its button on the taskbar. The desired window appears on top of any other open windows.

If you can't see your taskbar, try pressing Ctrl+Esc (hold down the Ctrl key and then press Esc). Your taskbar should spring up from the bottom of the screen.

Changing the Screen Colors

Microsoft spent a lot of time and effort designing the colors that you see on the screen when you start Windows. They also realized that individual tastes can vary widely. To help satisfy those individual tastes, they have included a whole bunch of color schemes for you to choose from. Here's how to change your Windows color scheme:

1. Choose Start⇨Settings⇨Control Panel. The Control Panel opens, as shown in Figure 4-4, displaying a bevy of Control Panel icons.

Figure 4-4: The Windows Control Panel.

2. Double-click — click twice in succession without moving the mouse — the Display icon to open the Display Properties dialog box.

3. Click the Appearance tab. The Appearance tab of the Display Properties dialog box jumps to the forefront.

4. Click the down arrow to the right of the box under the word *Scheme*. Use the scroll bar to view all the options in the list. When you click a color scheme, the top part of the Display Properties dialog box shows you how the selected color scheme looks.

5. When you find a color scheme you like, click OK. Windows applies the color scheme you choose immediately, and the Display Properties dialog box goes away.

6. Click the Close button to close the Control Panel window.

Setting the Date and Time

Your computer does a pretty good job of keeping track of the date and time, which may be important to you if you print documents that include a date. It also helps with file management. The computer automatically keeps track of the date and time you create and modify files.

Of course, the computer doesn't really know what time it is. It only knows what time you *say* it is. After you tell the computer the date and time, it diligently keeps track of them and displays the time in the bottom-right corner of the screen. Move your cursor over the time — but don't click — to see the date.

Here's how to change the date and time:

1. Choose Start➪Settings➪Control Panel.

2. Double-click the icon labeled Date/Time.

3. Select the month from the drop-down list.

4. Use the spinner controls — the up and down arrows — to select the year. Clicking the up arrow increases the value in the adjacent box. Clicking the down arrow decreases the value in the adjacent box.

5. Click on the appropriate day of the month.

6. To set the time, double-click on the hour, minute, second, or AM/PM indicator and type the new value, or use the spinner controls to reset the value.

7. Click OK to finish setting the date and time. Look in the lower-right corner of the screen to verify that you have set the time correctly. Move your cursor over the time to verify the date.

8. Click the Close button to close the Control Panel.

Many built-in PC clocks occasionally lose time. If you want your PC clock to be very accurate, check it once a week.

Getting Help from Windows

Windows has a rather extensive built-in Help system. To access it, click anywhere on the desktop and press F1. Make sure that you're at the desktop and not in application program when you press F1. Otherwise, you may instead get the Help window for the application that you're using.

The Windows Help window appears with three available tabs: Contents, Index, and Search. Click the Contents tab, if necessary. Help categories appear, denoted by a book icon. Click an icon to see a list of subjects in that category. The book opens to display a list of available topics, represented by a document with a question mark icon. Click any topic. Windows Help obediently displays help on the selected topic in the right pane of the Windows Help window. Feel free to resize or move the Help window as desired.

Don't be surprised if you click a book icon only to see a new list of books indented beneath it. Some categories, such as Introducing Windows 98, contain only other categories. Click one of these categories to see a list of Help topics.

If you don't want to browse through the Help Contents window, you may elect to click the Index tab and search through an alphabetically indexed list of Help topics. Here's how to find a specific topic in the index:

1. Click the Index tab to display the Help index.

2. Type the word that describes the topic on which you would like help. As soon as you start typing, the Help system automatically starts scrolling through the index to find the letter you type. Figure 4-5 shows the index in action. If you prefer not to type any words, you may use the scroll bar buttons to scroll through the list of Help topics.

Figure 4-5:   Windows Help topics.

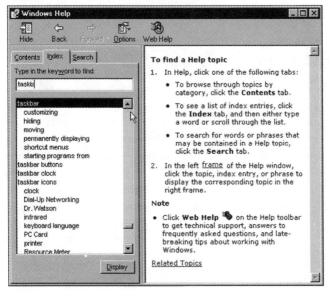

3. When you see the Help topic you want, click it. Windows Help displays the topic in the right pane.

Yet another way of obtaining help from Windows is to use the Search tab. The Search tab enables you to search for any word contained in the Help system. It's not restricted to the index of Help topics. Here's what to do:

1. Click the Search tab.

2. Type the word you want to search for. If you want help on maximizing a window, you may have more success if you type **maximize** rather than **window**. Just about every Help topic contains at least one reference to the word *window*.

3. Click the List Topics button. A list of topics matching your search criteria appears in the left pane of the Help window.

4. Click a topic to see it displayed in the right pane.

Shutting Down Windows

When should you shut down your computer? Good question. The debate rages on. Some people turn off their computers whenever they're going to be away for an hour or two. Some people leave their computers on all day and turn them off each night. Still others leave them on all week and turn them off for the weekend. A few people out there probably never turn off their computers. Today's energy saving systems make this an attractive choice for some. I, personally, prefer to turn off my computer when I know that I won't use it for several hours.

Usually, you can just switch off the monitor without shutting down the system unit. This saves power and minimizes those shadows that can burn into the screen. When you're ready to work again, you can switch the monitor on without waiting for the PC to completely restart.

Warning

When you decide to shut down your computer system, you must shut it down properly. That means giving Windows due warning that you're turning the computer off. Turning off the computer without first informing Windows can result in a loss of data and can also corrupt some of your Windows operating system files. This corruption may lead to a need to reinstall the operating system. Not much fun either way.

Here's how to shut down your computer:

1. Save any work and close any open programs.

2. Choose⇨Start⇨Shut Down.

3. Click the option button next to Shut Down. The option button is the small white circle to the left of the option. When you click an option button, a small black dot appears in the white circle.

4. Click OK. Your computer whirs and clicks for a few moments and then informs you that you can safely turn off your computer. At this point you may safely turn off the power to the computer. Note that some computers — notebooks especially, but also most newer desktop computers — may turn off automatically at this point.

CHAPTER 5

JOINING THE INTERNET

IN THIS CHAPTER

- Choosing an ISP
- Connecting to the Internet
- Surfing the Web
- Finding stuff with search engines
- Sending e-mail

Access to the Internet is the number one reason that new computer users acquire a PC. The reasons for wanting to connect to the Internet are varied — some people use it for research; some people want to communicate with others. A growing number of people use the Internet for shopping. You may want to do these things and more.

This chapter provides the briefest of introductions to some of the more common uses of the Internet and the World Wide Web.

Choosing an Internet Service Provider

Before you can surf the Web, you need to establish an account with an Internet service provider (ISP). An ISP has a fast connection to the Internet and an array of modems that you can dial up using your computer and modem. After your computer connects to the ISP's modem, you can access the Internet by sharing the ISP's fast connection.

When choosing an ISP, you need to decide whether to go with a national provider — an ISP that offers dial-up service no matter where you live in the United States — or a local provider — one that provides service to a small geographic area. As with most decisions, you have to weigh the pros and cons. Big, national ISPs can afford the latest and greatest equipment, while the smaller, local ISPs can offer more personalized service. The big guys also provide very good technical support.

In addition, many national Internet service providers send you a CD containing the software that you need to get started using the Internet. You simply place the CD in your CD-ROM drive and run a simple setup program. No need to worry about complicated network settings.

Surprisingly, cost isn't much of an issue. The going rate for unlimited dial-up Internet access is currently about $20 per month, which generally buys access to the World Wide Web and e-mail. Some ISPs provide space for a Web page and more than one e-mail account, which is handy if you have family members who want their own e-mail addresses.

Make sure that the ISP you choose has a local number for you to dial in to. If the number isn't local, you may have to pay long-distance charges for the time you spend connected to the Internet.

A good way to find an ISP is to ask your friends and neighbors who they use. Most people are willing to tell you about their ISP experience, especially if it isn't entirely positive. The Yellow Pages is another place to find a list of ISPs. Look under Computer Services. Stay clear of ISPs that require a long-term commitment, especially until you're sure that you like the service you receive from them. Most ISPs charge you on a month-by-month basis, allowing you to cancel your service at any time.

After you establish your account with the ISP, you receive a user name, a password, and a telephone number for your computer to call. You need these items to establish a connection to the ISPs computer, so make sure you don't lose them.

Connecting to and Disconnecting from the Internet

To connect to the Internet, you need a computer, a modem, some software, a phone line to plug the modem into, and an account with an ISP. You may use the software that comes with Windows, or, depending on the ISP you choose, you may use software provided by them. Either way, your ISP should provide detailed instructions for getting the software installed and set up on your computer.

Before you can *surf the Web* — in other words, use a Web browser to view Web pages or send e-mail — you have to tell your computer to make the connection to your ISP. How you do this depends on the ISP you have chosen. Most likely, you can double-click an icon on your desktop with your ISP's name on it.

Enter the user name and password provided by your ISP in the appropriate boxes and click the Connect button. The password you type shows up as a series of asterisks so that someone looking over your shoulder can't spy your password. Wait patiently while your computer calls the ISP's computer. Your modem may make some alarming noises as it tries to establish a connection with your ISP — this is normal. After a few moments, the noise stops, and your computer connects to the Internet. If you receive an error message stating that your user name or password is incorrect, try to connect again. Make sure that you enter the user name and password exactly as you received it from your ISP. Don't add any spaces or punctuation.

If you frequently receive a busy signal when attempting to connect, call your ISP and ask for an alternate number. If you receive busy signals on the alternate number, shop for a new ISP.

After you connect to the Internet, a small icon depicting two computers shows up in the lower-right corner of the Windows taskbar. Depending on your ISP — the Microsoft Network (MSN), for example — your Web browser may load automatically.

Right-click this icon when you want to disconnect from the Internet. In the Connect To dialog box that appears, click Disconnect, and your modem hangs up the phone. This dialog box, as shown in Figure 5-1, also displays the speed of your current connection.

Figure 5-1:   Windows tells you the status of your Internet connection.

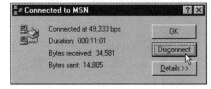

Unless you have two telephone lines, you can't make or receive phone calls while you're connected to the Internet. Any incoming callers receive a busy signal.

If your telephone has Call Waiting, the beeping for an incoming call may cause your modem to end your Internet connection. If this becomes a problem, ask your phone company how to disable Call Waiting.

Surfing the Web

After you connect to the Internet (see the previous section), double-click the icon for your Web browser on the Windows desktop. If you don't have an icon on the desktop, choose

Start➪Programs➪Name of your Web browser (most likely Microsoft Internet Explorer or Netscape Navigator). The Web browser opens, displaying your *home page,* which is simply the Web page that appears when you start the Web browser or click the Home button in the Web browser's toolbar. The home page is usually your ISP's Web site, but, as shown in Figure 5-2, you can set it to display any page you want.

Figure 5-2: Set your Web browser to your home page. This one is the publisher's favorite.

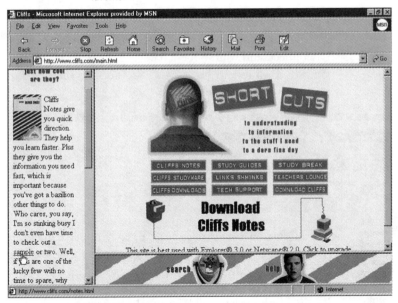

The *World Wide Web* — or the *Web,* for short — is a part of the Internet where you can use your Web browser to view Web pages. Web pages can consist of text, graphics, sounds, animation, and even full motion video. What makes the Web so easy to use is that Web pages can contain *hyperlinks* — text or graphics that, when clicked, take you to a different Web page either on the same Web site or to a different site altogether. A *Web site* is simply a collection of Web pages. Hyperlinks let you hop from one Web page to another without having to remember or type complicated Internet addresses.

Hyperlinked text is usually underlined, but telling if an image has a hyperlink is sometimes difficult. Your Web browser tells you when you're pointing at a hyperlink by changing the mouse cursor from the standard arrow to a hand with a pointing index finger.

When you click a hyperlink, the Web page you were viewing vanishes and a new Web page replaces it. If you decide you want to return to the Web page you were viewing, click the Back button on your Web browser's toolbar. Figure 5-3 shows a browser toolbar.

Figure 5-3:   The browser's toolbar helps you navigate the Web.

If you want to visit a particular Web page, you must type a Uniform Resource Locator (URL) — or, more simply, the Web address — for the Web page in the Web browser's Address box. A URL for a Web page always starts with `http://`. (With the newer Web browsers, you can omit the `http://`. For example, you can just type `www.cliffsnotes.com` and your browser takes you there.) After you type in the URL, press the Enter key. Your Web browser shortly displays the desired page.

If your Web browser displays the HTTP 404 – File Not Found error page instead of the Web page you wanted, check to make sure you typed the URL correctly. If you keep getting the error page, the page may not exist anymore, or the computer hosting the Web page may be temporarily down. Try the URL again later. If you're sure that you typed the URL correctly and that the Web page still exists, make sure that you're still connected to the Internet. You may have to reconnect to your ISP.

Some Web pages are too big to be displayed in a browser window. Use the browser's scroll bars — both vertical and horizontal — to see all of the Web page.

Finding Stuff with Search Engines

Getting information on a particular topic from a Web site is pretty simple if you happen to know the URL of the Web site that contains the information. But how do you find the URL to begin with? One way is to use an Internet search engine. A *search engine* is a Web site that enables you to enter a query and provides a list of hyperlinks to Web sites that contain the information that answers your query. Here are some of the better known search engines:

```
www.altavista.com
www.excite.com
www.goto.com
www.lycos.com
www.yahoo.com
```

Type the URL of a search engine in the Address bar of your Web browser and press Enter. Your Web browser displays the search engine's Web page. Then, type in some words that describe the information you're looking for and press Enter.

The search engine displays a list of hyperlinks to all the Web pages that match your search criteria. Click a hyperlink to view the listed Web page.

Don't be surprised if your search turns up hundreds, or even thousands, of Web pages. At the top of the list are the Web pages that contain the closest match to your criteria. The Web pages at the bottom of the list probably have little relation to the information you're seeking. Here are some tips to help narrow your search:

- Be as specific as possible. If you're looking for information on a 1954 Ford Customline, don't search for just the word *car*. Figure 5-4 shows a more specific search. You can always search again and make your search criteria less specific if the search doesn't turn up the information you're looking for.

Figure 5-4:   Searches can help you find what you want on the Web.

- If you're searching for a particular phrase, enclose the phrase in double quotes. Searching for Cliffs Notes turns up any Web page that contains both the word *Cliffs* and the word *Notes,* not necessarily next to each other. Putting double quotes around the phrase returns only those pages that contain the words *Cliffs Notes* together.

- Place a plus sign (+) in front of any word that must appear in the results. Don't put a space between the plus sign and the word.

■ Place minus sign (-) in front of any word that you want to exclude from your search. If you want to see Web pages about 1954 Ford automobiles, but you're not interested in Web pages that contain the word *truck,* enter **1954 Ford –truck** as the search criteria.

Be sure to scroll down to the bottom of the page to see all the results returned by the search engine. If you see a hyperlink labeled <u>Next Results</u>, <u>More Results</u>, or <u>Continue</u>, click the hyperlink to see the rest of the results.

When you have finished surfing the Web, click the close button in the upper-right corner of the Web browser window. If you want to disconnect from the Internet, double-click the small icon depicting two computers located in the right-hand portion of the taskbar. In the Connect To dialog box that appears, click Disconnect. This tells your modem to hang up the phone.

Working with E-mail

You send *electronic mail* — or *e-mail* — messages from your computer to someone else's computer via the Internet. Typically, you receive one or more e-mail accounts from your ISP when you sign up for Internet access; you must also have software to read e-mail, which your ISP probably provides.

Your *e-mail address* is like your postal address — it tells where your e-mail messages should be sent. Your e-mail address is usually your user name (for your ISP), followed by the @ symbol, followed by the domain name of your Internet service provider. For example, my e-mail address is `mccarterj@msn.com`. My user name is `mccarterj`, followed by the `@` symbol and the domain name of my ISP (`msn.com`). If you're not sure of your e-mail address, check with your ISP's technical support.

Many different e-mail programs are available, and they all do things a bit differently. The good news is that they also have the basics in common. You tell the e-mail program that you want to create a new message, to whom you would like to send it, type the message, and tell the program to send it. Your e-mail program sends the message to your e-mail server — usually at your ISP. Your e-mail server determines where to send the message from the address of the recipient, and it forwards the message to the recipient's e-mail server. The recipient's e-mail server places the message in a special folder that only the recipient can access. The message remains in this special folder until the recipient connects to the Internet, opens an e-mail program, and instructs the program to retrieve new messages.

Retrieving and reading e-mail

Here's how to retrieve and read e-mail using Microsoft's Outlook Express, a popular e-mail program that comes with Windows and Internet Explorer:

1. Connect to the Internet.

2. Choose Start⇨Programs⇨Outlook Express. The Outlook Express window appears. The folders pane of Outlook Express, shown in Figure 5-5, contains the following folders that can contain e-mail messages:

Inbox: This folder contains the e-mail messages that you have received.

Outbox: This folder contains the e-mail messages that you're waiting to send.

Sent Items: This folder contains a copy of all the e-mail messages that you send.

Deleted Items: This folder contains the e-mail messages that you delete. This folder empties when you exit Outlook Express.

Drafts: This folder contains e-mail messages that you have written but that aren't quite ready for you to send.

Figure 5-5: Outlook Express manages e-mail messages.

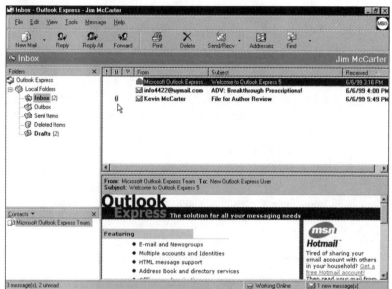

The first time you run Outlook Express, you can see a message from Microsoft welcoming you to Outlook Express. This message is installed with the program and provides useful information about Outlook Express.

3. To retrieve your e-mail, click the Send/Recv button located in the Outlook Express toolbar to tell Outlook Express to retrieve your e-mail. A window pops up, like the one shown in Figure 5-6, informing you that Outlook Express is checking for new e-mail messages. This window disappears when Outlook Express finishes checking for new e-mail.

Outlook Express places a closed envelope icon next to e-mail messages that you haven't opened. After you open an e-mail, Outlook Express changes the closed envelope icon to an open envelope icon.

4. To read a new message, click it. The message appears in the Preview pane below the message list. If you prefer to see the message in its own window, double-click the message.

Figure 5-6:   While Outlook Express receives e-mail, it tells you about the process.

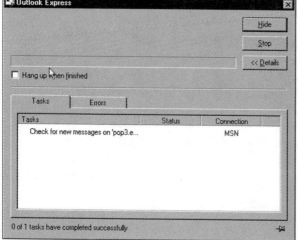

Sending e-mail

Follow these steps to send an e-mail message:

1. With Outlook Express open, click the New Mail button. Outlook Express opens a New Message window.

2. Click in the To box and type the e-mail address of the person to whom you're sending the message.

3. Click in the Subject box and type a brief description of the e-mail.

4. Click in the message window and type your message. Figure 5-7 shows a completed e-mail message.

5. When you finish typing your message, click the Send button. Outlook Express sends your e-mail message immediately.

If you don't know the e-mail address of the person to whom you want to send a message, you can try using a search engine. All the search engines listed in the section "Finding Stuff with Search Engines" earlier in this chapter — except www.goto.com — contain hyperlinks to help you find people and e-mail addresses. However, you may find it easier to just call the person and ask for the e-mail address!

Figure 5-7:   The e-mail box shows you the message and its address.

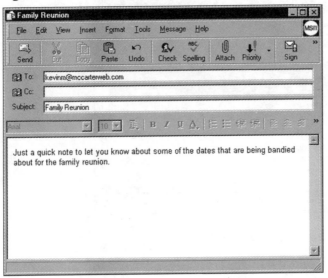

Attaching files to e-mail messages

In addition to sending text messages, most e-mail programs enable you to send attachments. An *attachment* is no more than a file that you send along with the e-mail message. The file may contain a picture, a word processing document, a recorded sound, or any other type of file.

Chapter 6 discusses the details of making and managing files. To attach a file to an e-mail message, follow these steps:

1. With Outlook Express open, click the Attach button in the New Message window. The Insert Attachment dialog box appears.

2. Navigate to where the file that you want to attach is and select the file.

3. Click the Attach button. A new box — labeled Attach — shows up under the Subject box, listing the file's name and size. When you send the e-mail message, the attached file goes with it.

You can easily tell when you receive an e-mail message with an attachment. Outlook Express displays a paperclip icon next to the message. To view the attachment, double-click the message to open it, and then double-click the filename of the attachment in the Attach box.

After you read an e-mail message, you have several options:

■ You can click the Close button in the message's upper-right corner to close the message and return to the message list.

■ You can send a reply to the author of the message by clicking the Reply button. Outlook Express opens a new message window with the To and Subject boxes filled in. Click in the message window and type your reply. Notice that the new message contains the text of the original message. Click the Send button when you finish typing your message.

■ You can send a copy of the message to someone else by clicking the Forward button. Outlook Express opens a new message window with the Subject box filled in. Type the address for the new recipient in the To box. If you wish, you may click in the message window to add your comments to the e-mail message. Click the Send button.

■ You can print the message by clicking the Print button. Outlook Express displays the Print dialog box. Click OK to print the message.

■ You can delete the message by clicking the Delete button. Outlook Express moves the message to the Deleted Items folder. When you exit Outlook Express, the message is permanently deleted.

■ You can view the previous message in the message list by clicking the Previous button. Outlook Express closes the current message window and displays the previous message.

■ You can view the next message in the message list by clicking the Next button. Outlook Express closes the current message window and displays the next message.

MANAGING YOUR FILES

IN THIS CHAPTER

- Opening files
- Saving files to disk
- Creating folders
- Copying and moving files
- Deleting files
- Recovering deleted files

A *file* is a collection of information stored on a medium that a computer can read. You can store files on your computer's hard disk, a CD-ROM disc, a floppy disk, a Zip disk, or even on a cassette tape (if you have the right kind of equipment to use the tape). Files can be divided into two basic groups:

- Data files (files that save your personal work)
- Program files (files that are put on the computer to make it operate)

This chapter introduces you to the basics of data file management. Although many of the techniques discussed in this chapter apply to both types of files, you are primarily concerned with data files.

Avoid using these file management techniques to change or delete program files. You can remove something that's necessary for your computer to work. If you want remove a program, look in its Help file for Uninstall instructions. Most programs will automatically delete themselves if you follow the Uninstall instructions.

Opening Files

You must open a file before you can view or modify its contents. The most common method of opening a file is to open the application program that you used to create the file and choose File⇨Open. Some programs can open files created in other programs — Microsoft Word can open files that were typed in many different programs.

Before you can open a file, you must know how to locate the desired file. Disks are organized in a hierarchical manner. A disk can contain one or more files and folders. Each folder can contain files and other folders. A folder that is contained within another folder is sometimes called a *subfolder*. Files that are stored on a disk but not in any particular folder are in the *root* of the disk.

Each file, folder, and disk drive has a name.

- Disk drives have names such as *A:* (for the first floppy disk drive) and *C:* (usually the first hard disk in a system). Disk drive names can range from A: to Z:.

- Files and folders can have much more descriptive names. A file or folder name can have up to 255 characters, including spaces and numbers, plus a three-letter file name *extension.* The filename and extension are separated by a period, like this: documentname.txt

  This extension tells Windows what type of program created a file. Examples are Melvin the Siamese Cat.bmp (a good name for a picture of the editor's cat) and Letter to the Editor.doc (a good name for a Microsoft Word document that tells the editor why no one wants to know the cat's name).

No two files in a single folder can have the same name. The same is true of folders.

Here's how to open a file in almost any program:

1. Choose Start⇨Programs⇨Name of program. Open any program you wish.

2. Choose File⇨Open.

The Open dialog box appears. Many programs also have an Open button on a toolbar, as pointed out in Figure 6-1; feel free to use that button, too.

Figure 6-1:   Many programs have an Open button to use existing files.

Open

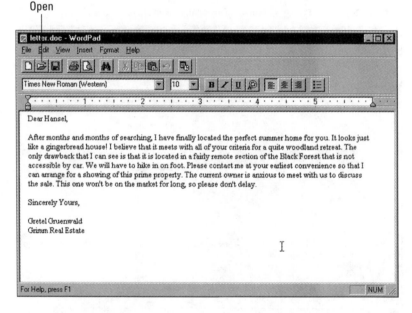

3. Navigate to where the file you want to open is on your hard drive.

Use the Look In drop-down menu to maneuver through the folders of your hard drive.

4. Double-click the filename.

The file appears in the program window.

Just about every program designed to run in Windows uses the same Open dialog box. The exceptions are programs such as Calculator and Solitaire, which can't open files.

Saving Files to Disk

Saving files to disk is sort of like putting your toys away when you finish playing with them. It keeps everything neat and tidy. It also ensures that you don't lose any changes you make to a file. Figure 6-2 shows a common way to save files.

Figure 6-2: To save most files, pull down the File menu and choose Save.

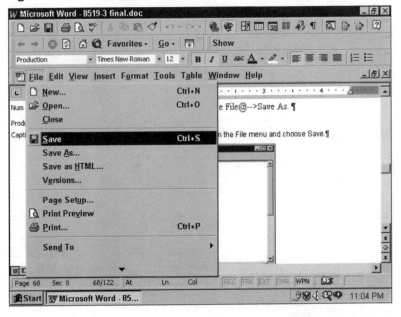

When you create a new document in an application program, the document doesn't exist in any permanent form until you save it to disk. Saving a document creates a new file. You simply tell the program to save the document, and then you give the newly created file a name. Here's how to save a new document in just about every kind of Windows program:

1. With a document open, choose File⇨Save As.

2. Type a descriptive name for your new file. Don't worry about adding a filename extension; the program automatically adds the appropriate extension to the end of the name.

3. Navigate to where you want to save the document with the Save In drop-down list.

You probably want to save most of your documents in the My Documents folder, as shown in Figure 6-3.

4. Click Save to save the new file to the destination you chose in Step 3. The Save As dialog box goes away, and you return to the program window. Now that you have given the file a name, the program window displays the filename in its title bar.

Figure 6-3:   The Save As dialog box lets you decide the name and location of your files.

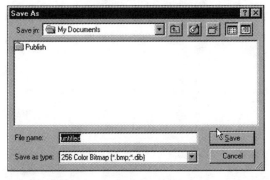

Renaming Files

At some point, you may decide that you want to change the name of the file. You may think of a name that more accurately reflects the contents of a file, or you may have mistyped the name of a file when saving it. Whatever your reason for changing a filename, the procedure is fairly easy.

Here's how to change a filename using Windows Explorer:

1. Choose⇨Start⇨Programs⇨Windows Explorer. Windows Explorer opens, showing you a list of files and folders.

2. In the left pane of Windows Explorer, select the drive that contains the file you want to rename. The contents of the drive appear in the right pane of the Explorer window, as shown in Figure 6-4. If the file you want to rename is located in a folder, double-click that folder.

Figure 6-4: Windows Explorer gives you access to the files on your computer.

Left pane   Right pane

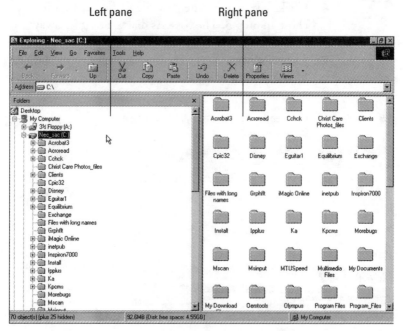

3. Click once on the file you want to rename.

4. Choose File⇨Rename. The name of the file is highlighted, as shown in Figure 6-5.

Figure 6-5:   While you rename the file, the part you are changing is highlighted.

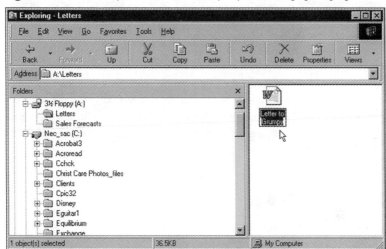

5. Type the new name for the file and press Enter.

Copying and Moving Files

Moving and copying files is as easy as dragging the file from one folder to another. Here's how:

1. Choose Start⇨Programs⇨Windows Explorer. Windows Explorer opens, showing you a list of files and folders.

2. To move a file, drag the file from the right pane of Windows Explorer to the new folder in the left pane. When the folder you want to move the file to is highlighted, release the mouse button.

3. To copy a file, select the file in the right pane of Windows Explorer and, while holding down the Ctrl key, drag the file to the new folder. The mouse cursor displays a small plus (+) sign to indicate that you're copying and not moving the file.

You can copy and move multiple files by holding down the Ctrl key while selecting the files in the right pane of the Explorer window. Then drag the files to the new folder. Be sure to hold down the Ctrl key while dragging if you want to copy the files instead of moving them.

You can copy and move folders just as easily as files. Remember that when you move or copy a folder you also move or copy the folder's contents, including any subfolders and files that they contain.

Deleting Files

Deleting files in Windows is easy. Some say too easy. Simply select the files that you want to delete in Windows Explorer and press the Delete key.

Windows displays the Confirm File Delete dialog box asking if you really want to send the selected files to the Recycle Bin. To send the selected files to the Recycle Bin, click Yes. If you decide that you don't want to delete the files, click No.

Recovering Deleted Files

When you tell Windows to delete a file, Windows doesn't actually erase the file. Instead, Windows puts the deleted file in a special container on the desktop called the Recycle Bin. If you accidentally delete a file, you can probably recover it by fishing it out of the Recycle Bin. I say "probably" because the Recycle Bin is only so big (usually about 10 percent of your hard disk). When the Recycle Bin fills up, it starts throwing out the oldest items — the first items that were placed in it — to make room for any new files that you delete. So, even though you can probably recover files that you delete, be careful that you don't delete any files that you really need.

Here's how to "recycle" a deleted file:

1. Double-click the Recycle Bin icon on the desktop. The Recycle Bin opens and displays your deleted files, as shown in Figure 6-6.

Figure 6-6: The Recycle Bin holds files that will be permanently removed from your computer.

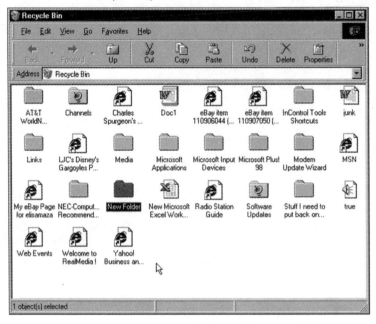

2. Select the file or files that you want to recover. Hold down the Ctrl key while selecting multiple items.

3. Choose File⇨Restore. The selected files disappear from the Recycle Bin and return to the folder you deleted them from.

Only files deleted from your local hard disk are sent to the Recycle Bin. If you delete a file from a removable disk, the file is permanently deleted.

CHAPTER 7

PUTTING BUILT-IN PROGRAMS TO WORK

IN THIS CHAPTER

- Writing a note
- Sending a fax
- Making quick calculations
- Painting a picture
- Playing a music CD
- Playing Solitaire

Microsoft, in an attempt to make Windows the Swiss Army knife of operating systems, includes a medley of small applications — called applets — with Windows. These applets don't provide all the functionality of some of the "big" applications, but they can be quite useful. This chapter introduces you to some of the more helpful features.

Writing a Note

If you need to type a document but don't have a big word processing package, such as Microsoft Word, you may want to take a look at Windows WordPad. It doesn't offer the power of Microsoft Word, but it works fairly well for typing quick letters and other simple documents.

To launch WordPad, choose Start⇨Programs⇨Accessories⇨WordPad.

WordPad opens with a blank document and a blinking *insertion point* — that blinking black line — in the upper-left corner of the document window. The insertion point shows you where the next character you type will appear. Don't confuse the insertion point with the mouse pointer. The mouse pointer changes appearance depending on the portion of the screen that you're pointing at. Point at the title bar or one of the toolbars, and the mouse pointer becomes the familiar arrow pointer. Move the mouse pointer into the document window, and it changes to the I-beam pointer. Figure 7-1 shows the insertion point and mouse pointer in WordPad. After you type some text, you can move the insertion point by clicking the mouse to where you want to place the insertion point.

Figure 7-1: The WordPad window shows the text that you are writing.

Typing in WordPad is similar to typing on a typewriter, but you want to keep some differences in mind. One big difference is that you don't need to press Enter at the end of each line. Just keep typing. WordPad automatically starts a new line when you fill up the current line. This feature is called *word wrap*. Of course, you can start a new line whenever you like by pressing Enter. When you press Enter in WordPad, you begin a new paragraph.

If you make a mistake when typing, you can delete characters by pressing the Delete or Backspace keys. The Delete key removes the character to the immediate right (or in front) of the insertion point. Pressing Backspace removes the character to the immediate left of (or behind) the insertion point. If you hold down either key, you end up rapidly removing additional characters.

Changing text appearance

WordPad provides some features for jazzing up the appearance of your documents. You can change the font type, size, and style. The *font* — sometimes called a *typeface* — describes the basic shape of each character. By default, WordPad uses the Times New Roman font.

Here's how to change the font of your text:

1. Highlight the text by clicking and dragging over it.

2. Click the down arrow next to the Font box and select a new font from the drop-down list, as shown in Figure 7-2. The font for the selected text changes.

You can also change the font before you start typing. Just select a font, as in Step 2 in the previous numbered list. Anything you type afterward appears in the new font. Existing text isn't affected.

In addition to changing the font type, you can change the size of the font. Here's how:

1. Highlight the text that you want to change.

2. Click the down arrow next to the Font Size box and select a font size. You may also click in the Font Size box and type a value if you don't want to select from the drop-down list. The font size of the selected text changes.

Figure 7-2: After you select text, you can change its typeface.

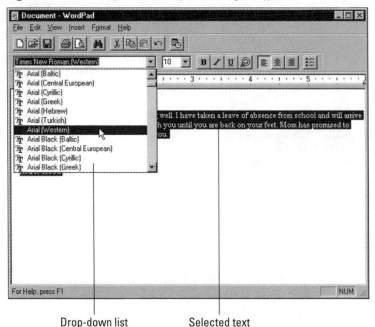

Drop-down list   Selected text

In addition, you can change the style of the font. Your options are bold, italic, and underline. Here's what to do:

1. Highlight the text that you want to change.

2. Click the Bold, Italic, or Underline buttons on the toolbar. These buttons act as a toggle. Click them once to turn them on; click them a second time to turn them off. You can apply one or all three of these styles to the selected text.

Inserting the time and date

Another nice feature that WordPad offers is the ability to insert the current date and time. Follow these steps:

1. Move the insertion point to where you want to insert the date or time.

2. Click the Date/Time button at the end of the toolbar. The Date and Time dialog box appears.

3. Select the format for the date that you desire, as shown in Figure 7-3, and click OK. The current date now appears in your document.

Figure 7-3: Choose how you want the date displayed in your document.

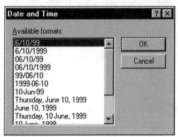

4. To insert the time, you must scroll to the bottom of the Available formats list, where you can choose between 12-hour (AM/PM) and 24-hour (military) formats.

Changing the color of text

If you have a color printer, you can add some color to your WordPad documents. Here's how:

1. Highlight the text that you want to make a different color.

2. Click the Color button — the one with the *A* and the artist's palette.

3. Click a color from the drop-down list. Your text changes to the selected color.

Printing a document

To print your document, make sure that your printer is connected and turned on. Also make sure you load it with paper. Click the Print button — you can't miss this one; it has a picture of a printer on it. (Some people say it looks more like a typewriter, but it's supposed to be a printer.) Your computer thinks for a few moments, and then your printer spits out a copy of the current document.

Saving a document

When you finish typing your document, you probably want to save a copy of it for future use. Follow these steps:

1. Click the Save button — the one that looks like a floppy disk. The Save As dialog box appears, as shown in Figure 7-4.

Figure 7-4:   Use the Save As dialog box to name your document.

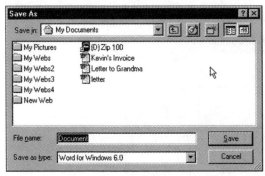

2. Type a descriptive name for your document.

3. Navigate to where you want to save the document. Don't forget where you put it!

4. Click the Save button.

Exiting WordPad

When you finish with WordPad, be sure to exit the program by choosing File⇨Exit. If you haven't saved any changes you've made to the current document, WordPad prompts you to do so. Click Yes to save the current document; click No to exit WordPad without saving.

Sending a Fax

If you have a fax modem installed in your computer, you can use the fax software included with Windows to send faxes directly from your computer. No need to print the document first and then take it to a fax machine. Follow these steps to send a fax:

1. Choose Start⇨Programs⇨Accessories⇨Fax⇨Compose New Fax. The first window of the Compose New Fax wizard appears, as shown in Figure 7-5.

Figure 7-5:   Use this dialog box to compose a fax.

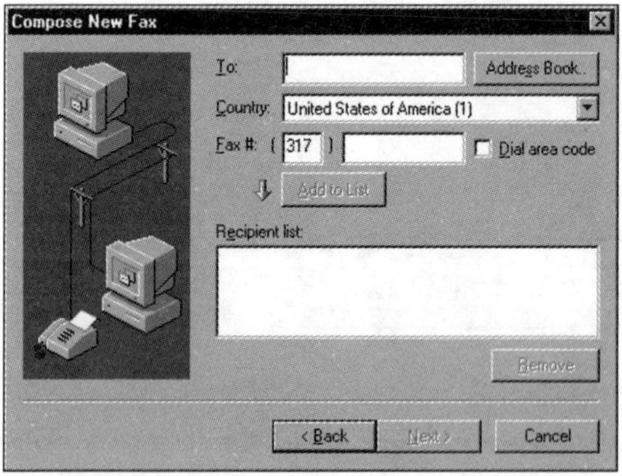

2. Type the name of the person you're sending the fax to in the To box.

3. Type the fax number in the Fax # box. Be sure to enter an area code if the recipient's area code is different from yours.

4. Click the Add to List button. The name that you typed in the To box shows up in the Recipient List box. You can send the same fax to multiple recipients by repeating Steps 1 through 3.

5. Click the Next button when you finish entering recipients. The second window of the Compose New Fax wizard appears.

6. If you want to send a cover page with your fax, click the option button next to "Yes. Send this one:". Then choose the cover page you want to send from the list below. Microsoft Fax automatically fills in the recipient information on the fax cover sheet. If you do not want to send a cover sheet, click the option button next to No.

7. Click Next.

8. Type a Subject and Note for your fax. If you want to fax a document that you have already typed and saved to disk, you may elect to leave the Subject and Note boxes empty.

If you want the note to start on the cover page, be sure to click the Start note on cover page check box.

9. Click Next. Microsoft Fax gives you the option of faxing a document that you have saved on disk. If you don't want to fax a file that is saved to disk, skip to Step 12.

10. To fax a file from disk, click the Add File button. The Open File to Attach dialog box appears.

11. Select the file that you want to fax and click Open.

12. Click Next to see the last window of the Compose New Fax wizard. Microsoft Fax informs you that it is ready to send your fax.

13. Click Finish to send your fax.

Making Quick Calculations

Windows includes a nifty little calculator program tucked away in the Accessories folder. Just choose Start➪Programs➪Accessories➪Calculator. The Windows Calculator appears, as shown in Figure 7-6, ready to do your arithmetic for you.

Figure 7-6:   The Windows Calculator is included with the Windows operating system.

This program functions just like your run-of-the-mill — and, in this case, free — handheld calculator. To enter numbers, you can use the keyboard or click the on-screen number pad with your mouse. The operator buttons — + to add, - to subtract, * to multiply, / to divide, and = for equals — work just the same as on a handheld calculator.

For more advanced functionality, choose View➪Scientific. The Calculator window expands to show new buttons and features. To return to the less complicated calculator that you started with, choose View➪Standard.

Click the Close button in the Calculator window's upper-right corner to exit the program. The Calculator doesn't have a File menu with an Exit command.

Painting a Picture

As the saying goes, "a picture is worth a thousand words." Most of the pictures I draw are worth a thousand laughs. If you have a yearning to explore your creative side, or if you have a need to create a simple illustration, Microsoft Paint may be able to help.

To get started, choose Start⇨Programs⇨Accessories⇨Paint to launch the program.

You can divide the Paint window into four parts. At the top of the window are the title bar and menu. The left side of the window holds the toolbox with various drawing and selection tools. The large white area is your canvas. The bottom of the windows contains the color palette and, below that, the status bar. Figure 7-7 shows the Paint program window.

Figure 7-7:   The Paint accessory allows you to draw on your computer screen.

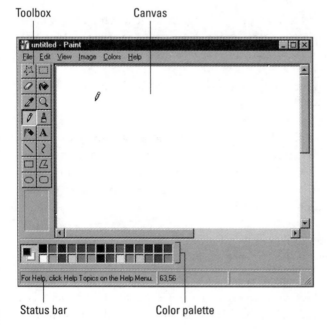

Toolbox   Canvas

Status bar   Color palette

Point to any tool in the toolbox, and a small yellow box appears, displaying the name of the tool. Look in the status bar at the bottom of the Paint window to see a description of the tool.

Before you draw, select a color from the color palette at the bottom of the Paint window.

Click a drawing tool, and then click and drag in the picture area to draw. To draw freehand, select the Pencil, Brush, or Airbrush tool. To draw a predefined shape, select the Line, Curve, Rectangle, Polygon, Ellipse, or Rounded Rectangle tool.

You can fill a shape with color by selecting a color from the color palette, clicking the Fill With Color tool — the one that looks like a paint bucket — and clicking inside a shape.

Click the Eraser/Color Eraser tool to erase part of a picture.

To add text to your drawing, click the text tool. Click in the drawing and start typing. You can change the text font, size, and style by choosing View⇨Text Toolbar.

To print your masterpiece, choose File⇨Print and click OK in the Print dialog box.

Close the Paint program by choosing File⇨Exit. If you haven't saved your work, Paint gives you the opportunity to do so. Click No to exit the program without saving. Click Yes to bring up the Save As dialog box. Type a name for your creation and click Save.

Playing a Music CD

If your computer has a CD-ROM drive, a sound card, and speakers, you can use it as a very expensive CD player. Place a music CD in the drive, close the door, and just listen. Your music CD probably starts playing automatically. If it doesn't, you can launch the CD Player program by choosing Start⇨Programs⇨Accessories⇨Entertainment⇨CD Player.

Here's how to play a music CD with the CD Player:

1. After inserting the CD in the CD-ROM drive, click the Play button in the CD Player, which is shown in Figure 7-8.

Figure 7-8:   Play music from your computer's CD drive.

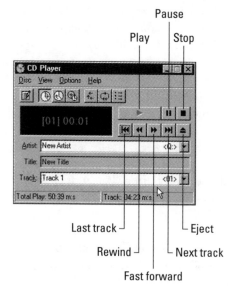

Pause

Play   Stop

Last track

Rewind   Next track

Eject

Fast forward

2. To adjust the volume, click the Speaker icon in the lower-right corner of the Windows taskbar. In the resulting Volume control, drag the slider control up to increase the volume or down to decrease the volume.

To quickly turn the sound off without stopping the CD, click the Mute box in the Volume control. Click the Mute box a second time to restore the sound.

3. When you're done listening to the CD, click the Stop button to stop playing the CD. This resets the CD Player to track one — the beginning of the CD. To stop the CD without resetting it to track one, click the Pause button. Click the Play button to resume listening to the CD.

If you don't know what a button does, point to it with the mouse pointer. A description pops up in a yellow box.

By default, the CD Player plays each track on your CD in order and then stops. Click the Continuous Play button to have the CD Player continue playing until you click the Stop or Pause buttons. Click the Random Track Order button to have the CD Player play each track randomly.

If you want to listen to your CD while you work on other things, click the Minimize button. CD Player shrinks to a button on the taskbar and continues to play. Click the CD Player on the taskbar to restore the CD Player window to its previous size.

To change CDs, click the Eject button. Put in the new CD and click the Eject button again to close the drive. Click Play to listen to the new CD.

When you finish listening to CDs, click the Close button in the upper-right corner of the CD Player window or select Exit from the Disc menu.

Playing Solitaire

For those of you who need to brush up on your mouse-handling skills, Microsoft includes a program called Solitaire.

Okay, so it's really a game. Nothing wrong with having some fun while you learn. Figure 7-9 shows a game in progress.

To launch Solitaire, choose Start⇨Programs⇨Accessories⇨Games⇨Solitaire. Solitaire obediently shuffles and deals the cards for you. If you have ever played Solitaire, you should have no trouble with this program. If you don't know how to play or need a refresher course, choose Help⇨Help Topics.

Figure 7-9:   Solitaire allows you to practice pointing, clicking, and dragging. Really.

You move the cards by dragging them to where you want them. By the way, Solitaire doesn't let you cheat; if you try to move a red card onto another red card, Solitaire politely returns the card to its original location!

After you finish one game (either by winning or getting stuck), choose Game⇨Deal to start a new game. If you'd rather Exit the game, just click the Close button in the upper-right corner.

CHAPTER 8

PUTTING OTHER APPLICATIONS TO WORK

IN THIS CHAPTER

- Writing a letter in Microsoft Word
- Creating a To-Do list in Microsoft Works
- Putting together a flyer in Microsoft Publisher

Microsoft Windows comes with many useful features, but it can't do everything. That's why so many software packages are available. This chapter takes a quick look at three popular programs that you may want to explore further.

Creating a Letter in Microsoft Word

At the most basic level, WordPad and Word are very similar programs. Both enable you to type and manipulate text, save your work, and print the results. The difference between the two is that Word offers many more features and options.

This section shows you how to create a professional-looking letter in Microsoft Word using one of Word's built-in templates. A *template* is simply a document that's already formatted and has boilerplate (or stand-in) text. You replace the boilerplate text with your own text, and you have a nice, professionally designed document without having to spend a lot of time formatting it.

Follow these steps to create a letter (I assume you already have Microsoft Word installed on your computer):

1. Choose Start⇨Programs⇨Microsoft Word. A blank window appears.

2. Choose File⇨New. The New dialog box appears.

3. Click the Letters & Faxes tab. A list of templates appears.

4. Select Contemporary Letter. A preview of the document appears in the Preview box.

5. Click OK to open the template. The template with boilerplate text appears in a new window.

After you have the template open, go ahead and start writing your letter. Here's how:

1. In the upper-right corner of the document, click the text that reads "[Click here and type return address]," as shown in Figure 8-1. The text highlights automatically. Type your return address, pressing the Enter key after each line.

Figure 8-1:   Microsoft Word is a common word processing program in the professional community.

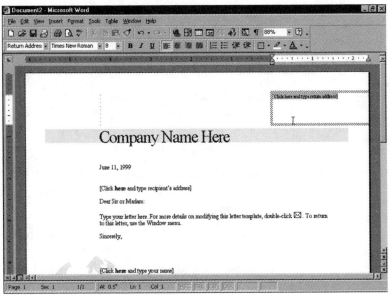

2. Highlight the text that reads "Company Name Here" in large type and type the name of your company. If this is a personal letter, you can enter your name in place of the company name, or you can delete the text.

Remember

You can select text with the mouse or arrow keys.

To select text with the mouse, put the screen pointer at one end of the text you want to select, then hold down the left button of the mouse. Drag the mouse to put the screen pointer at the other end of the text you want to select; then release the left button of the mouse.

To select text with the arrow keys, start by using the arrow keys to put the insertion point at one end of the text you want to select, then hold down the Shift key. Use the arrow keys to put the insertion point at the other end of the text you want to select; then release the Shift key.

3. Click the text that reads "[Click here and type recipient's address]." Type the recipient's address, pressing the Enter key after each line.

4. Select the text "Sir or Madam" and type a new salutation, if you want.

5. Select the paragraph that begins with the sentence "Type your letter here" and begin typing your letter.

Remember

Don't press the Enter key at the end of each line. Microsoft Word automatically begins a new line when you reach the end of a line. Press Enter only when you want to start a new paragraph.

6. When you finish typing the body of the letter, click the text that reads "[Click here and type your name]" and type your name.

7. Click the text that reads "[Click here and type job title]" to select the text and type in your job title. If you prefer not to include your job title, select the text and press Delete.

8. Click the text that reads "[Click here and type slogan]" and type your company's slogan. If your company doesn't have a slogan or you don't want a slogan to appear on your letter, press Delete.

That's all there is to it. You may print the letter by clicking the Print button in the toolbar. Your printer immediately begins printing a copy of your missive, complete with the fancy globe watermark.

If, after using the template to create your letter, you're not satisfied with the result, you can change the formatting just as if you typed the letter from scratch. Here are a few things you can do:

■ Change the font type by selecting the text and clicking the down arrow next to the Font box. Pick a font from the drop-down list, and your selected text changes to the new font.

■ Change the font size by selecting the text and clicking the down arrow next to the Font Size box. Choose a font size from the drop-down list, and your selected text changes to the new font size.

■ Add Bold, Italic, or Underline style to the text by selecting the text and clicking the corresponding button on the toolbar. Click the Bold, Italic, or Underline button a second time to turn off the style.

After you format your letter to your liking, you can save it by clicking the Save button on the toolbar. In the Save As dialog box (shown in Figure 8-2) that appears, type a new name for your document or accept the default, and click the Save button.

Figure 8-2: After you finish writing a letter, name it and save it.

Creating a To-Do List in Microsoft Works

Many new computers come with preinstalled software packages. Microsoft Works is an *integrated software package* — one program that combines the features and functionality of two or more programs — that's frequently installed on new PCs. Microsoft Works combines a word processor, a spreadsheet program, a database management program, and a communications program into one package.

Here, I show you how to create a To-Do list using Microsoft Works (I assume you already have Microsoft Works installed on your computer):

1. To launch Microsoft Works, choose Start⇨ Programs⇨Microsoft Works⇨Microsoft Works.

2. If necessary, click the Task Wizards tab.

3. Click the gray diamond next to Business Management to expand the category.

4. Scroll down the list until you see the To Do List item. Click To Do List and then click OK. The Works Task Launcher appears.

5. Click the button next to Yes, Run the Task Wizard. The Works TaskWizard appears, as shown in Figure 8-3.

Figure 8-3: Microsoft Works allows you to create lists of your daily jobs with a few steps.

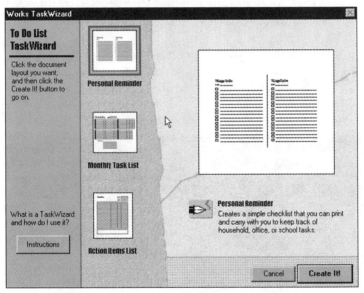

6. Select the type of To Do List that you want to create.

7. Click the Create It! button. A blank To Do List appears. You can click on the blank lines and type your list of To-Do items, or you can print the blank form and enter the information by hand.

8. Click the Print button in the toolbar to print a single copy of the To-Do list.

9. If you want to save the document, click the Save button. In the Save As dialog box that appears, type a name for the new document and click Save.

Putting Together a Flyer in Microsoft Publisher

This section shows you how to create a flyer for a garage sale using Microsoft Publisher. Microsoft Publisher lets you create professional-looking publications with a minimum of effort, even if you don't have any design experience.

To get yourself started, follow these steps (I assume you already have Microsoft Publisher installed on your computer):

1. Choose Start⇨Programs⇨Microsoft Publisher. The Microsoft Publisher Catalog appears with the Publications by Wizard tab open, as shown in Figure 8-4.

Figure 8-4: Microsoft Publisher includes lots of forms you can make your own.

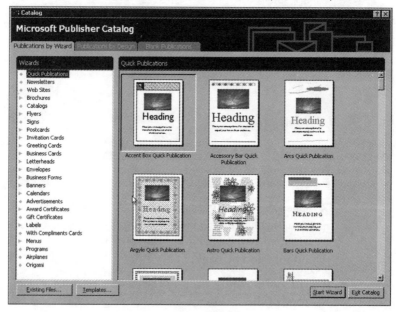

2. Click the Flyers category in the Wizards list. The Flyers category expands.

3. Click Sale under Flyers. The right pane of the Microsoft Publisher Catalog shows the available Sale Flyers.

4. Scroll down until you can see the Garage Sale Flyer and click the Garage Sale Flyer document preview.

5. Click the Start Wizard button located in the lower-right corner of the window. The first panel of the Flyer Wizard appears.

6. Read the introduction, and then click Next. The second panel of the Flyer Wizard appears.

7. If you plan to print the flyer on a color printer, select one of the 60 available color schemes. Otherwise, accept the default Black & White color scheme and click Next.

8. Decide whether you want to include a placeholder for the customer's address. Because this is a flyer for a garage sale, accept the default — no — and click Next.

9. Select the personal information set that you want to use in the publication. Accept the default and click the Finish button.

After you set up your flyer document, you can start customizing the information about your garage sale. Here's what to do:

1. Click the Hide Wizard button to hide the Flyer Wizard panel.

2. Click the date to highlight it and type the date of your garage sale. If the type is too small for you to read, press the F9 key to magnify the page.

3. Click the time to highlight it and type the time for your garage sale.

4. Select the "Describe your location by landmark or area of town" placeholder text and type some text to tell people how to find your garage sale.

5. Select the placeholder text in the bottom-left corner of the flyer and list the kinds of items that you plan to sell.

6. Select the placeholder text in the bottom-right corner of the flyer and list your most interesting items for sale.

7. Click the Print button on the toolbar to print a copy of your garage sale flyer.

8. Click the Save button on the toolbar to save a copy of your garage sale flyer, and exit Microsoft Publisher.

CHAPTER 9

PRINTING

IN THIS CHAPTER

- Choosing a printer
- Installing printer drivers
- Printing

The paperless office has yet to arrive. And until it does, you're probably going to want to print some of those wonderful documents that you create. This chapter reviews the different types of printers that are available and explains how you get them ready to print.

Choosing a Printer

While enhancements in printer technology seem to occur everyday, only three commonly used categories of printers still exist: dot matrix, inkjet, and laser. Which printer is right for you depends on the type of documents you need to print, how many documents you print, and how fast you want them to print.

Dot-matrix printers

Dot-matrix printers — also known as *impact printers* — work by striking a ribbon against the paper with a set of 9 or 24 wires. These printers print one character at a time and are usually pretty slow. While this type of printer is fairly inexpensive, it's very noisy and offers relatively poor print quality.

Dot-matrix printers have pretty much gone the way of the manual typewriter, so why would you want one? Dot-matrix printers excel at two types of printing. The first is printing multipart forms. You know the type — you keep the yellow copy; they keep the white and pink copies. This type of form requires an impact printer. The second type of print job that dot-matrix printers do well is printing banners. Most dot-matrix printers can handle continuous feed paper — something that most inkjet and laser printers can't handle. Some dot-matrix printers can print in color. Unless you need to print multipart forms or banners, you probably want to consider an inkjet printer.

Inkjet printers

Inkjet printers have almost entirely replaced the aging dot-matrix printer. Inkjet printers are inexpensive — they start at about $90 — and are relatively quiet. They print by spraying ink onto the page. The only sound they make is that of the print head moving back and forth across the page.

Earlier versions of inkjet printers were very slow, but modern ones can print in excess of eight pages of text per minute. They can even print letter-quality text and photo-realistic color images. Although the printers themselves are relatively inexpensive, their supplies can be costly. Printing graphics-intensive documents uses up color ink cartridges quickly, and you must print on special — translation: expensive — inkjet paper for the best results. Another drawback is that, because the printer sprays the ink onto the paper, the ink can smear if you touch the print before it dries. Most home users print to inkjet printers.

Laser printers

Once upon a time, you found *laser printers* only in large offices in which many people could share them to help off-set their high price tags. Today, with personal laser printers available for well under $300, laser printers often appear in the home office environment.

Laser printers are usually very fast and provide high-quality output. In addition, laser printers can print thousands of pages before you must replace the toner cartridge. If you need to print large quantities of black and white documents, the laser printer is a good bet for you. You can get color laser printers, but they're probably too expensive for the average home user. Current prices for color laser printers start at about $1,500 — more than the cost of many new computers.

Installing Printer Drivers

Before you can print to a printer, you must properly connect it to the computer. You also have to make sure that your computer and the printer speak the same language. You accomplish this by installing a piece of software known as a printer driver. A *printer driver* is a set of instructions that tells Windows how to access the printer's functions. Every printer should come with a printer driver created by the printer's manufacturer.

Here's how you introduce your computer to your printer. Make sure that you have your Windows CD handy when performing the following steps. If a CD is included with your printer, you need that CD, too.

1. Choose Start⇨Settings⇨Printers. The Printers window appears with an icon for each printer installed on your computer, as shown in Figure 9-1.

2. Double-click the Add Printer icon to start the Add Printer Wizard.

3. Click Next.

4. Select Local printer to tell Windows that the printer is attached to your computer.

Figure 9-1: The Printers icons allow you to control printers connected to your computer.

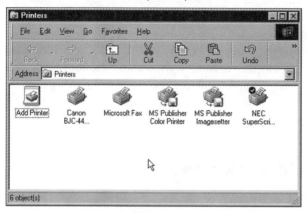

5. Click Next.

6. Select the company that made your printer from the Manufacturers list, and then select the correct model of your printer from the Printers list.

7. Click Next.

8. Select the LPT1: option to tell Windows that the printer is connected to your printer port.

9. Click Next.

10. Type a name for your printer or accept the default name. If you plan to use this printer most often, click Yes to set it as your default printer. If you have more than one printer and this printer won't be the primary printer, click No.

11. Click Next.

12. Click Yes and then click Finish to have Windows print a test page. If Windows can't find the required files on your hard disk, Windows asks you to place your Windows CD in the CD-ROM drive. Click OK after you have done so.

13. After Windows prints the test page, click Yes if the page printed successfully.

14. Click the Close button in the upper-right corner of the printer window. Now you're all set to print!

Printing

The easy, no-nonsense way to print in most Windows programs is to use the Print button — the one with the picture of a printer — on the toolbar. Clicking this button usually results in printing one copy of the current document to the default printer, using the default printer settings.

If you want more control over the way a document prints — which printer it prints to, the number of copies, and so on — choose File⇨Print to bring up the Print dialog box (see Figure 9-2).

Figure 9-2:   The Print dialog box controls your printer every time you print.

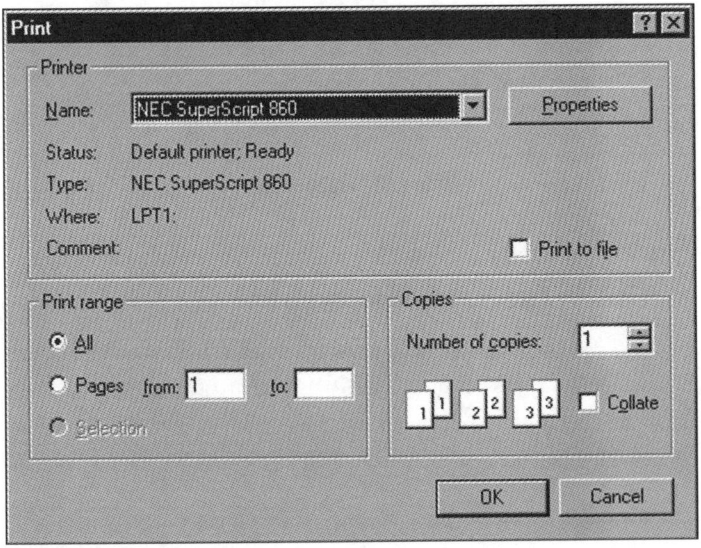

Before you print your document, use Print Preview to make sure your document will print the way you want it to. Print Preview can save you money on ink cartridges and paper. Just click the Print Preview button on the toolbar — the one with the paper and magnifying glass — or choose File⇨Print Preview.

The Print dialog box

The Print dialog box has a variety of options for you to play around with, depending on the program you're printing from. Check these out:

■ To print to a printer other than the default, click the down arrow next to the Name box and select a printer.

■ To change the number of copies you want to print, use the arrows next to Number of copies. You can also type in the number of copies you want.

■ To change which pages you want to print, choose from the options in the Page Range area.

■ If you're printing more that one copy of a multipage document, click the Collate check box to save yourself a lot of sorting and collating time.

Click OK in the Print dialog box to print your document with your new settings.

The Page Setup dialog box

You can access additional printer settings from the Page Setup dialog box. Just choose File⇨Page Setup to call up the Page Setup dialog box. The changes you make in this dialog box remain in effect until you change them again.

The following options vary depending on your printer and the program that you're printing from.

- To print on different-sized paper, click the down arrow next to the Size box and choose a new paper size. Make sure that the size you choose matches the paper that you loaded into your printer.

- To switch between multiple paper sources, select which one to use from the Source drop-down list. This option is especially handy if you have a printer with plain paper in one tray and letterhead paper in another.

- To change the page orientation, choose either landscape or portrait. Portrait orientation is what you're used to — the shorter edge of the paper is at the top and bottom. Landscape turns the paper on its side — the longer edge is on the top and bottom. Use landscape for documents that are too wide to fit on a portrait-oriented page.

- To change how much blank space is between the edge of the paper and the text of the document, type new values in the Top, Bottom, Left, or Right boxes of the Margins area.

TROUBLESHOOTING

IN THIS CHAPTER

- Solving start-up problems
- Thawing out your frozen system
- Finding lost files
- Solving printing problems

If you use your computer long enough, sooner or later you'll encounter a problem that leaves you scratching your head. This chapter offers some basic troubleshooting tips to help you out of those spots.

Start-up Problems

Here are some common obstacles you may encounter when you first boot up your Windows PC, as well as a few fixes.

The computer doesn't start

You turn on the computer, but absolutely nothing happens. Make sure that you plugged in the power cord. If you plugged the computer into a surge protector — a good idea — make sure that you plug in and turn on the surge protector. Also make sure that you turn on any wall switches that control the outlet that the computer plugs into.

Nothing on the screen

You turn on the computer and it makes all the usual noises, but the screen remains blank. Check to make sure that the monitor is plugged in and turned on. Also, check to see if the brightness and contrast controls are turned all the way down. Turn them back up to see the display. If these hints don't help, you may have a defective monitor or video card. Your monitor or video card may need professional help.

The dreaded "invalid system disk" message

You turn on the computer, expecting to see the wonderful world of Windows, only to be confronted with the following message:

```
Invalid system disk
Replace the disk, and then press any key
```

This message almost invariably means that you left a floppy disk in the floppy disk drive. Remove the disk and press the space bar; Windows should start shortly. If Windows doesn't start, you may have a dead hard disk, which is very bad news if you don't have a backup copy of any important data on the drive. If you do keep a backup, then get yourself another hard disk and restore your files from the backup.

Errors on the hard disk

You receive a message at startup telling you that one or more of your disk drives may have errors on it. This message usually means that you (or somebody) didn't shut down the computer properly the last time it was used. Just be patient while Microsoft ScanDisk gives your hard drive a physical. Windows starts automatically when ScanDisk finishes. In the future, to avoid this message and having to wait while Scan-Disk runs, choose Start⇨Shut Down when you want to turn off your PC.

A jumpy mouse pointer

The mouse pointer appears on the screen, but when you move the mouse, the cursor jumps all over the place. Your mouse is probably dirty. Turn the mouse over. Remove the ball from its belly and wipe the ball with a clean cloth. Check to see if any gunk is in the mouse hole. If cleaning the mouse doesn't solve the problem, you may need to buy a new mouse.

System Freezes

You are busily working away when suddenly your computer stops working. Here's what you do (in this order):

1. Move the mouse around to see if the mouse pointer is active. If the mouse pointer doesn't move, then your system is most probably frozen.

2. Press Ctrl+Esc. That is, hold down the Ctrl key while you press and release the Esc key. This should cause the Start menu to appear. If it doesn't, go to Step 3. If the Start menu does appear, use the arrow keys to select Shut Down and press Enter. The Shut Down Windows dialog box appears; click Enter again to shut down.

3. Go get a cup of coffee before you do anything drastic. Sometimes your computer is thinking really hard about something. When you come back, you may find that the computer is working fine again.

4. After waiting a considerable amount of time, press Ctrl+Alt+Del. That is, hold down the Ctrl and Alt keys while you press and release the Del key. This should bring up the Close Program dialog box containing a list of currently running programs.

5. Look for a program with the words *Not responding* following the program name.

6. Select the not-responding program and click the End Task button. This should close down the offending program and return you to the Windows desktop, where you can restart your computer properly.

7. If Step 6 doesn't work, press Ctrl+Alt+Del again while the Close Program dialog box is open. This should cause your computer to restart. If you have any unsaved documents open, you unfortunately lose the unsaved data in those documents.

If you've gone through this entire procedure and you still can't shut down or restart your computer, you're going to have to take the most drastic step of all: turning off the power to the computer, either by the power switch or by unplugging the computer from the wall. Wait at least thirty seconds or so before you turn the computer on again. Be prepared to go through the ScanDisk routine (which I explain in the previous section).

Finding Lost Files

You spend hours working on a file to get it just right. You save the file to your hard disk so that you can return to it later only to find that, when you try to open the file again, you can't remember where you put it.

First, open the program that you used to create the lost file. Look under the File menu at the Recently Used Files list, as shown in Figure 10-1. If the file is on the list, click the filename to open it. Then, after the file opens, choose File⇨Save As and make a note of where you saved the file.

Figure 10-1: The list of recently-used files can save you lots of time and worry when you look for a file.

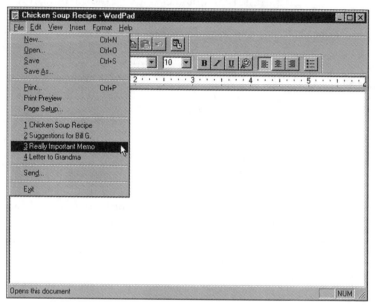

If your lost document doesn't appear on the Recently Used Files list, you can still search for the file using the Windows Find utility. Here's how:

1. Choose Start⇨Find⇨Files or Folders. The Find dialog box appears, as shown in Figure 10-2.

Figure 10-2: Find: All Files searches your whole computer disk for files.

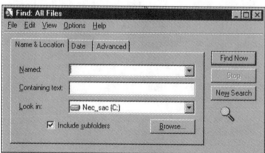

2. Do one of the following:

Type the name of the file in the Named box. If you can only remember part of the name, type that portion of the name in the Named box.

If you can't recall the name of the file, but you can remember some of the words contained in the document, type the word or words in the Containing Text box. If possible, pick a word that's unique to the file you're searching for — this narrows the search and saves you lots of time in finding the correct file.

If you can't recall the filename or the file's contents, but you have a pretty good idea when you last used the file, click the Date tab, as shown in Figure 10-3. If you last used the file in the past 24 hours, click the Find All Files option and select Last Accessed from the drop-down list. Then click During the Previous Day(s).

You can also search for files accessed between two specified dates or within a certain number of months. Simply choose whichever option you want and fill in the dates.

Figure 10-3: You can fine-tune your search.

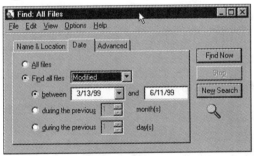

3. Click the Find Now button. The Find dialog box expands to show the filenames that match your search criteria, as shown in Figure 10-4.

Figure 10-4: The files that match your search are listed.

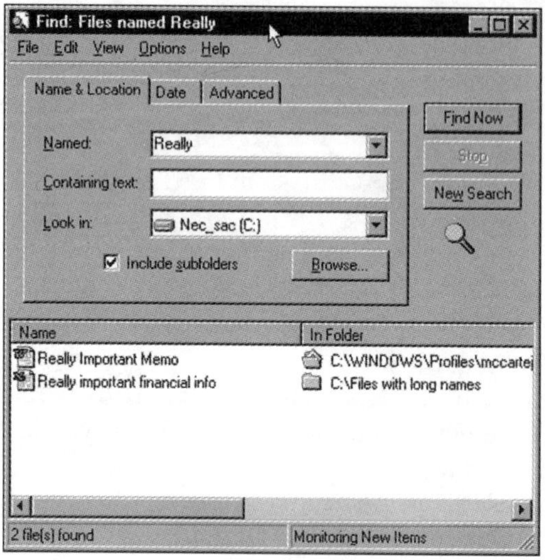

4. To open a file listed in the Find dialog box, double-click the filename. The file opens in the program that you used to create it.

If you want to cancel a search in progress, click the Stop button. To start over with a new search, click the New Search button. A confirmation box appears (shown in Figure 10-5), alerting you that your current search parameters will disappear. Click OK.

Figure 10-5: A confirmation box gives you an extra chance to protect your information.

The Advanced tab of the Find dialog box enables you to search for files of a given type. If, for example, you know that the file is a PowerPoint presentation, click the down arrow next to the Of Type box and select Microsoft PowerPoint presentation, as shown in Figure 10-6.

Figure 10-6:   You can search for files made by a particular program.

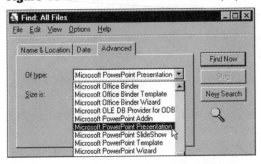

The Advanced tab also lets you search by file size. You can search for files that are at least a certain size or at most a certain size. Select either At Least or At Most from the Size Is box. Enter a number in the KB box to indicate the size in kilobytes.

You can combine options from all three tabs to help narrow your search even more. To close out of the Find dialog box, choose File⇨Close or click the Close button in the upper-right corner.

Resolving Printer Problems

You send a document to the printer, but nothing comes out. Here are some suggestions for finding the trouble:

■ Check for loose cables. Make sure that you firmly connect the printer cable to both the printer and the computer. Use the retaining clips that keep the printer cable attached to the printer.

- Make sure that you plug in the printer's power cord and turn on the printer. Some printers have an Online or Ready button. Press this button to ensure that the printer is listening to the computer.

- Make sure that you properly load paper in the printer. Sometimes, when paper is improperly loaded in the tray, the paper sensor doesn't realize that the paper is there.

- Try printing from a different program. Perhaps the problem is with the program and not the printer.

- Check to make sure you didn't pause the printer. Choose Start⇨Settings⇨Printers. Then double-click the icon representing the printer you're trying to print to. If you see the word *Paused* in the title bar, as shown in Figure 10-7, of the printer window, choose Printer⇨Pause Printing to restart printing.

Figure 10-7: Use this dialog box to check on files while you wait for them to print.

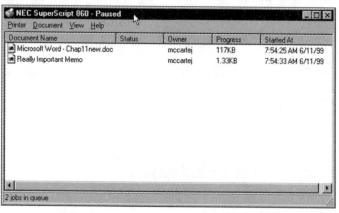

Document Name	Status	Owner	Progress	Started At
Microsoft Word - Chap11new.doc		mccartej	117KB	7:54:25 AM 6/11/99
Really Important Memo		mccartej	1.33KB	7:54:33 AM 6/11/99

2 jobs in queue

- Make sure you're sending the print jobs to the right printer. In the program, choose File⇨Print. Double-check the name of the printer.

- Change the print driver. If your printer prints a bunch of garbage whenever you send a print job, you may be using the wrong printer driver. Select the correct printer from the Name box in the Print dialog box.

- Change the ink or toner cartridge if the output quality is low. Refer to your printer's manual for instructions.

If all else fails, call your printer manufacturer's technical support number. Make sure that you have the printer model and serial numbers handy.

CLIFFSNOTES REVIEW

Use this CliffsNotes Review to practice what you've learned in this book and to build your confidence in doing the job right the first time. After you work through the review questions, the problem-solving exercises, and the fun and useful practice project, you're well on your way to achieving your goal of using your PC confidently.

Q&A

1. How should you exit from an application that's running?

   a. Push the Reset button.

   b. Save your work and then close the program.

   c. Click the lower-left corner of your screen.

   d. Turn the computer off.

2. What happens when you click a menu name?

   a. Nothing; you have to use the keyboard to use menus.

   b. A menu that's open on-screen closes.

   c. A menu appears, showing commands you can click.

   d. b. and c.

3. How do you start a program?

   a. Use the mouse to highlight its name and then press Enter.

   b. Find the program in your computer's directory of folders and double-click its name.

   c. Type the program's name at the command prompt and press Enter.

   d. All of the above.

4. What happens first when your computer boots up?

   a. A built-in program starts the operating system.

   b. Your user interface appears on the screen.

   c. The computer prints out a test document.

   d. The document you're working on appears.

5. How often should you save your work?

   a. Every 10 to 15 minutes.

   b. Every two or three hours.

   c. Weekly.

   d. Never; computers are completely reliable.

6. What is a boot disk?

   a. A disk that comes in a hard plastic case.

   b. A disk that contains startup files for emergency use.

   c. A disk you must always put in the drive after you boot up.

   d. A disk that contains user's instructions for your system.

7. Which of these methods can you use to transfer files from the C: drive to a floppy-disk drive labeled B:?

   a. From drive C:, select the files you want and then double-click the first one.

   b. Open a window for each drive, select files in the drive C: window, press and hold down the left mouse button, move the mouse pointer over to the drive B: window, and release.

   c. Open a window for the B: drive, use the mouse to select files in the drive C: window, and then type **copy these files to B:**.

   d. Write down the names of the files you want to copy, close the user interface, reboot the computer, and then type **copy to B:** at the command prompt, followed by the filenames.

8. How can you determine whether an application is appropriate to run on your PC?

   a. Read about it in a computer magazine.

   b. Check the system requirements on the software box.

   c. Know which peripherals are installed in your system.

   d. All of the above.

9. What is the best approach to buying a PC?

a. See it advertised on TV at a great price and go buy it.

b. Buy as many features and devices as you can afford.

c. Always buy state-of-the-art and upgrade every 6 months.

d. Decide what you want to use a PC for, find the software that will do it, and look for a PC that runs the software well.

10. How do you "unfreeze" a program that refuses to respond?

a. Press Ctrl+Alt+Del.

b. Press Esc repeatedly.

c. Switch to another window and try a command from there.

d. Type as fast as you can until something happens.

Answers: (1) b. (2) d. (3) d. (4) a. (5) a. (6) b. (7) b. (8) d. (9) d. (10) a.

Scenarios

1. You finished a letter to a friend and saved it, but when you open your word processor, you can't find it. How can you find your letter?

_____

_____

2. You bring home a new laser printer for your computer and connect it to your system, but when you try to print a document, nothing happens. What can you do to fix the problem?

_____

_____

Answers: (1) Use your computer's file-management utility program (such as Windows Explorer or File Manager) to show you the directory tree; use the utility's Search (or similar) command to hunt for the file name of your letter; when you find the letter, save it to a specific folder (most Windows users can use the My Documents folder). (2) Make sure the correct device driver for your printer is installed; the printer should include a disk that has the driver program and instructions that tell you how to install it.

Visual Test

Which of the ports in back of your computer connect it to the printer, the monitor, the mouse, and the Internet? Sketch them and check your cables to make sure they are correct for each port.

Consider This

What tasks are you doing now that would go faster and easier on a computer? Which tasks are easier if you use pen and paper? What kind of work is best suited to a computer?

Practice Project

You want to update your résumé and give it a professional look. Use your word processor to do the job:

1. Start your word processor.

2. Start a new document in your word processor.

3. Place a clean copy of your old résumé on a copy stand next to your screen.

4. Type the text of your résumé into your on-screen document.

5. Use your word processor's paragraph-formatting commands to left-align your résumé list items and to center-align your section headings.

6. To preserve the work you've done so far, save your document with the heading `myresume.doc`.

7. Use your mouse or keyboard to select the entire document and then use your word processor's character-formatting commands to select a businesslike font for your résumé.

8. Spell-check your résumé and edit it for grammar and accuracy.

9. Save your résumé twice more — once to a directory on your hard drive (most Windows users can use the My Documents directory), and once to a formatted floppy disk so you have a backup copy. Then print out and file the updated résumé.

CLIFFSNOTES RESOURCE CENTER

The learning doesn't need to stop here. CliffsNotes Resource Center shows you the best of the best — links to the best information in print and online about personal computing. And don't think that this is all we've prepared for you; we've put all kinds of pertinent information at www.cliffs-notes.com. Look for all the terrific resources at your favorite bookstore or local library and on the Internet. When you're online, make your first stop www.cliffsnotes.com, where you'll find more incredibly useful information about using PCs.

Books

This CliffsNotes book is one of many great books for PC users from IDG Books Worldwide, Inc. So if you want some great next-step books, check out some of these other publications:

Upgrading & Fixing PCs For Dummies, 4th Edition, by Andy Rathbone, guides you step-by-step to figuring out what's broken and how to fix it. With these easy-to-follow instructions, you'll be able to take care of all those nagging problems and install all the hardware you need. IDG Books Worldwide, Inc., $19.99.

Teach Yourself the Internet and World Wide Web VISUALLY, by Ruth Maran, shows you (in full color) what e-mail, mailing lists, newsgroups, chats, and the World Wide Web have to offer for you. IDG Books Worldwide, Inc., $29.99.

Job Searching Online For Dummies, by Pam Dixon, presents winning strategies from a seasoned online pro to help you find the right job fast. IDG Books Worldwide, Inc., $24.99.

The Internet For Windows 98 For Dummies, by Margaret Levine Young, John Levine, Jordan Young, and Carol Baroudi, leads you step-by-step through the ever-expanding Internet. Go find out what this Internet stuff is about! IDG Books Worldwide, Inc., $19.99.

You can easily find books published by IDG Books Worldwide, Inc., in your favorite bookstores, at the library, on the Internet, and at a store near you. We also have three Web sites that you can use to read about all the books we publish:

`www.cliffsnotes.com`

`www.dummies.com`

`www.idgbooks.com`

Internet

Check out these Web resources for more information on your PC.

Microsoft Windows Update, http://windowsupdate. microsoft.com takes you directly to the latest official news from Microsoft about Windows 98 and the updates, service packs, and patches you can use to fix bugs.

Microsoft Dowload Center, www.microsoft.com/ msdownload takes you to the Download Center of the Microsoft Web site, where you can get free downloadable programs to enhance Windows 98 and its related applications.

Windows Users Group Network, www.wugnet.com/ win98/resources is the home of the Windows Users Group Network (WUGNET). Here you can find a wealth of unofficial, practical information about using all versions of Windows.

Next time you're on the Internet, don't forget to drop by www.cliffsnotes.com. We created an online Resource Center that you can use today, tomorrow, and beyond.

Magazines and Other Media

PC World, at your local newsstand, shows you the latest news and tips for your PC and how changes in the software industry affect it. Sample its wares at www.1pcworld.com.

Windows Magazine covers the world of Windows: hardware, software, buying, testing, comparing. Visit its Web site at www.winmag.com.

Send Us Your Favorite Tips

In your quest for knowledge, have you ever experienced that sublime moment when you figure out a trick that saves time or trouble? Perhaps you realized you were taking ten steps to accomplish something that could take two. Or you found a little-known workaround that achieved great results. If you've discovered a useful tip that helped you use your PC more effectively, and you'd like to share it, the CliffsNotes staff would love to hear from you. Go to our Web site at www.cliffsnotes.com and look for the Talk to Us button. If your tip is selected, we may publish it as part of *CliffsNotes Daily*, our exciting and free e-mail newsletter. To find out more or to subscribe to a newsletter, go to www.cliffsnotes.com on the Web.

INDEX

COMING SOON FROM CLIFFSNOTES

Online Shopping

HTML

Choosing a PC

Beginning Programming

Careers

Windows 98 Home Networking

eBay Online Auctions

PC Upgrade and Repair

Business

Microsoft Word 2000

Microsoft PowerPoint 2000

Finance

Microsoft Outlook 2000

Digital Photography

Palm Computing

Investing

Windows 2000

Online Research

COMING SOON FROM CLIFFSNOTES
Buying and Selling on eBay

Have you ever experienced the thrill of finding an incredible bargain at a specialty store or been amazed at what people are willing to pay for things that you might toss in the garbage? If so, then you'll want to learn about eBay — the hottest auction site on the Internet. And CliffsNotes *Buying and Selling on eBay* is the shortest distance to eBay proficiency. You'll learn how to:

■ Find what you're looking for, from antique toys to classic cars

■ Watch the auctions strategically and place bids at the right time

■ Sell items online at the eBay site

■ Make the items you sell attractive to prospective bidders

■ Protect yourself from fraud

Here's an example of how the step-by-step CliffsNotes learning process simplifies placing a bid at eBay:

1. Scroll to the Web page form that is located at the bottom of the page on which the auction item itself is presented.

2. Enter your registered eBay username and password and enter the amount you want to bid. A Web page appears that lets you review your bid before you actually submit it to eBay. After you're satisfied with your bid, click the Place Bid button.

3. Click the Back button on your browser until you return to the auction listing page. Then choose View⇨Reload (Netscape Navigator) or View⇨Refresh (Microsoft Internet Explorer) to reload the Web page information. Your new high bid appears on the Web page, and your name appears as the high bidder.